KICKING IN THE WIND

The real life drama of a small-town football club

Derick Allsop

HEADLINE

First published in 1996 by
HEADLINE BOOK PUBLISHING

10 9 8 7 6 5 4 3 2 1

British Library Cataloguing in Publication Data

Allsop, Derek
    Kicking in the wind
    1. Rochdale Association Football Club 2. Soccer teams –
England – Rochdale 3. Soccer – England
    I. Title
    796.3′34′09427392

ISBN 0 7472 1927 3

Typeset by Palimpsest Book Production Limited,
Polmont, Stirlingshire
Printed and bound in Great Britain by
Mackays of Chatham PLC, Chatham, Kent

HEADLINE BOOK PUBLISHING
A division of Hodder Headline PLC
338 Euston Road
London NW1 3BH

Contents

To my ever dependable back three:

Sue, Natalie and Kate

Acknowledgements

It would not have been possible to produce a book like this without the total co-operation, forbearance and good humour of everyone at Rochdale Football Club; so to the directors, management, players, staff, relatives and supporters I extend my heartfelt thanks. I also wish to express my appreciation of the assistance given me by the local Press corps, the invaluable service provided by the *Rochdale Observer*, and the diligent Steven Phillipps, whose book about his beloved club, *The Survivors*, proved a precious source of information and inspiration.

Introduction

It is 3.40 on a Wednesday morning and Rochdale AFC's team coach pulls on to the forecourt at the club's ground and headquarters, Spotland. A round trip of more than 570 miles and a working day of almost 17 hours are over, and Rochdale have nothing to show for the ordeal. They went to Torquay brimming with optimism but had a player sent off and lost 1–0. Those bare facts, however, cannot begin to convey the emotional turmoil being endured by the solemn figures stepping on to the tarmac, wearily fumbling for car keys.

David Kilpatrick, the club's chairman, would come closer to achieving that, reflecting: 'I can live with Rochdale getting beaten, for Christ's sake. My frustration comes from the fact that we are not in a position to do the things we want to do. That was an horrendous day – I got to bed at five to four and thought to myself "What a complete and utter waste of time that was – stuck in traffic, didn't do anything properly, the game was crap, we lost and came back home."'

Doing things properly, the way the big clubs do them – travelling the day before the match and staying overnight, or even flying – costs money, the kind of money Rochdale and many others in the lower reaches of English football do not have and do not even dream of having. The Third Division of the Endsleigh League is the factory floor of the game, where diligent tradesmen endeavour to stave off injury and competition long enough to make a living, buy a comfortable semi and run a second-hand car. The fame and riches of the Premier League might as well belong to a different planet.

A club and town like Rochdale does not merely epitomise this 'other' football world, it provides a parody of the sporting and social environment at this level of the game. Kilpatrick concedes: 'Rochdale – the very name sounds boring. It sounds like a bloody clog town and a mill town . . . It really is a one-eyed, one-horse town where nothing happens.'

And yet, within the inevitable constraints, a club like Rochdale can still have its ambitions and motivations, whatever the aspirations of the civic fathers. Kilpatrick offers a developing Spotland as a rare focal point for local pride and is not alone in believing a club such as his is essential to the structure of football in this land. The supporters, too, yearn for greater things – a Cup run, the play-offs, even promotion. Faith and hope will forever bond all football people.

Alas, usually they have been left disappointed and disillusioned, resignation and fatalism taking over minds and hearts. Some 135 fans also made that trek to and from the West Country. As definitions of loyalty go, that takes some beating. The story has been much the same throughout Rochdale's existence. They have never been higher than the old Third Division and have been stuck in the bottom division for the past 22 years. Survival alone has been hailed as victory against a backdrop of financial crises and boardroom wrangles.

It is exactly 100 years since this 'one-eyed, one-horse town' – then simply and unambiguously part of Lancashire, long before the invention of Greater Manchester – fielded its first representative football team. The enterprise of Rochdale Athletic Club, like that of Rochdale Town, proved short-lived, but in 1907 Rochdale Association Football Club was born, dressed in black and white stripes, raised in the Manchester League and accepted by the Football League, as a member of the Third Division (North), in 1921.

Heroes of those distant days included the captain, David Parkes, who routinely completed his match-day preparations by downing a couple of pints in a pub near Spotland. The team had to go without their half-time break during a match in the North-East in order to catch the train home.

Rochdale was subjected to its own depression in the thirties, relying on a range of fund-raising efforts to continue. The town's most famous and celebrated daughter, Gracie Fields, helped from a distance and a former player-turned-comedian, Harry Mallalieu, gave a concert for the cause. The Supporters' Club organised collections, although a 'shilling fund' appeal was perhaps taken too literally. It raised precisely . . . a shilling.

Rochdale, in common with the rest of English football, enjoyed a boom period after the Second World War. An FA Cup tie, against Tommy Lawton's Notts County, in 1949, attracted Spotland's record attendance, 24,231 (receipts: £2,285 9s 6d). Rochdale could never quite boast such illustrious names in their teams, although they can claim a kind of distinction in having had on their books Charles Hurst and Alan Ball, fathers of England's World Cup winners, Geoff and Alan junior. They had a centre-half called Errington Ridley Liddell Keen (conveniently better known as Ike) and one Calvin R C H Symonds, a taxi driver from Bermuda. The management and coaching staff has included Harry Catterick, Joe Fagan, Bob Stokoe, Jimmy Greenhoff and Eddie Gray.

Would-be comedians appear to have been as common as would-be chairmen. Tommy Cannon joined the board of Rochdale AFC around the time his partner, Bobby Ball, became a director of Rochdale Hornets Rugby League Club. Cannon briefly had the chair and left amid little laughter. The title 'Mr Rochdale' was the preserve of Fred Ratcliffe, the League's youngest chairman in 1953. A year later Spotland had floodlights – before Old Trafford, Anfield and Goodison Park.

In the aftermath of Cannon's departure, the social club was renamed the Ratcliffe Arms and the football club again teetered on the brink of financial ruin. More ingenious money-raising schemes were dreamed up, more changes were forced in the board-room and the long-mooted ground-sharing deal with Hornets was agreed. Eventually David Kilpatrick, once an undertaker, became chairman for a second time and assumed responsibility for resurrecting 'Dale. Through the nineties, guided by the financial director, Graham Morris, he has pursued a policy of pragmatism at the club. It has, at times, exasperated the manager and the fans, but it has dragged Rochdale from the abyss and sustained their League status.

Mick Docherty, Rochdale's latest manager, reluctantly accepts the financial restraints. He does not have an open cheque; he does not even have a contract. But he has a job and he knows that if he does it as well as can be expected he will keep it. If he does not, he is out. He reluctantly accepts that, too. This is where and when the fantasy ends – and another kind of football life begins.

CHAPTER ONE

Remember the Stick-on Smile

Friday 7 July 1995: men's semi-finals day at Wimbledon. England are struggling against the West Indies at Edgbaston and menacing clouds are disturbing the morning sunshine at Spotland as Rochdale Association Football Club confronts another season competing in the nation's No.1 sport. Uncertainty – meteorological or otherwise – is customary in this part of the land but Mick Docherty, the manager, offers a summery countenance to match his shorts.

He arms himself for any eventuality with a piece of advice from his father, Tommy, a manager who encountered eventualities previously unimagined. 'My dad always said you could have the world on your shoulders, the bank manager might be after you, your wife might be having an affair and your kids may be ill, but as soon as you hit that front door you get on the stick-on smile, because you can't afford to let them see you down in case it rubs off on them.'

Football can exhaust any mortal's sense of humour, but at this level the constraints would drive you to submission unless you had no desire for, or prospect

1

of, an alternative way of life. Many are driven away. Others, like Mick Docherty, the directors, the players, the coaching and administrative staff here at this modest Third Division club, simply get on with it.

In the reception area at Spotland, Docherty (complete with stick-on smile) greets the chairman, David Kilpatrick, a large bespectacled man, and his long-time colleague, Graham Morris, the financial director, a tall, lean man. They are meeting for a 'pre-season chat', a euphemism for a mini crisis talk. They all know the discussions will be dominated by money, or to be more precise, the lack of it. But then money, or the lack of it, dominates just about every facet of life at a small football club.

Life should have been made considerably more comfortable by the ground-sharing scheme with Rochdale Hornets Rugby League Club. The overall policy of Spotland is governed by the Stadium Company, Denehurst Park (Rochdale) Ltd, which has representatives from the Football and Rugby Clubs, and the Council. The clubs each have 45 per cent of the shares in the Company, the Council 10 per cent. However, almost inevitable differences have caused resentment.

Behind the office door of the Football Club, to the left, you hear complaints of unneighbourly behaviour, and behind the office door of the Rugby Club, to the right, you will doubtless hear similar grumbles. The Football Club feel they are unfairly burdened by the additional cost incurred complying with safety and licensing requirements in their sport, which, they argue, ultimately benefit both clubs. One football official sneers: 'I wouldn't trust them as far as I could throw them.' The rugby people denounce their housemates as whingers.

Docherty, Kilpatrick and Morris head for the door ahead of them, turn right, stroll down the corridor, then turn left to the manager's office. Docherty settles behind his desk, facing Kilpatrick, Morris and racks of kit. 'We keep them in here for security reasons,' Docherty explains.

Already Morris, a local accountant, has been busying himself attending to basic requirements. 'We had £1 million of work done that was supposed to have been planned properly and what have we got? Just two urinals in the men's toilet. It's bloody chaos in there on match days. This is what it's really like at this end of the League – worrying about the toilets.'

They have other pressing business, such as finding the money to pay the players' wages, including 'loyalty bonuses'. The club's commercial department endeavours to maintain a year-round flow of funds and clubs tap into the League pool, but income from matches remains the lifeblood and the last home match was in April. The directors, loath to go to the bank for a loan, face up to the alternative – dipping into their own pockets. 'Let's just bloody pay it,' Morris recommends. Five of them subsequently cough up £5,000 each.

Docherty has lined up a goalkeeper but would also appreciate a couple of full-backs and a little more oomph up front. The expressions on the faces of Kilpatrick and Morris convey scant encouragement. 'See how you get on with the keeper' is the concession.

Docherty suggests he ought to have a weekly budget of £8,000 for wages and be free to operate his own pay structure. The bill is already about £7,800, he estimates, with the top wage of £500 a week. Some players are on £400 but the bulk of them are on £300. Docherty says that proposition has been rejected, as has his request for a contract. He has learned to adjust the stick-on smile and go to work. That work begins in earnest again on Monday morning, when the players report for pre-season training. Ten o'clock. Sharp.

By the appointed hour this warm Monday morning Spotland is abuzz like a school on the first day of term. Docherty was on the road at 8 o'clock, picking up the new kit from Frank Casper, another former Burnley player. He organises the piles of tops, shorts and socks with the pride and care of a housemaster. His philosophy is: 'If you set the standards it's up to the players to respond, and if they ever moan we can tell them "Look, we do all we can for you, now you do your bit".'

He is joined in his office by Jimmy Robson, yet another former Burnley player, a goalscorer in the 1962 FA Cup final, and all-round man of the game. He confirms what his tan tells you: 'Got back from holiday yesterday. Crete. Brilliant.' Next into the ever more crowded office is Dave Bywater, a gangling, affable man, more ruddy than tanned. His longish locks earned him the nickname David Soul way back. Must be a mystery to his present charges. Robson and Bywater are responsible for the club's emerging talent, Bywater being specifically involved in the development of the Centre of Excellence. Yes, they do have one at Rochdale.

Docherty maps out the day: 'The lads are getting weighed first, always like to do that, just to check on them, then they'll have a bit of a pep talk from the chairman. When that's done we'll have a run, oh, three miles or so, through the woods, a break for lunch, then some ball work in the afternoon.'

The chairman arrives and duly marches towards the dressing room, where the players, already changed into their smart training gear, are waiting, sitting on the benches, shaking their calf and thigh muscles, the way all players feel obliged to do. Kilpatrick is beaten to the first words by one of the team wags: 'We know, we're all available.'

Kilpatrick enjoys the joke, and the one about his tie, and proceeds, pointing out that although there is a perception that the club do not really want to progress and that they would be happy to go down to the Vauxhall Conference, 'that's absolute rubbish.' He goes on: 'You lads who don't live locally are lucky because you don't have to put up with the garbage we get thrown at us all the time round here. Our message to you lads is "stuff it up 'em, stuff it up the whingers". We started well last year and I know we could have done better. I just hope and want you to sustain it this year.'

As the players head for the woods, the seniors in cars, the juniors in a minibus, a YTS boy clad in one of Manchester United's shirts – the green and gold one – is called back by the chairman. 'Don't you ever wear that here again,' he barks. You can be sure he won't.

An older player receives a warmer reception. He is Ian Gray, the goalkeeper Docherty wanted. Gray had a spell on loan here last season and now has been transferred from nearby Oldham Athletic, for a fee of £20,000.

The convoy drives along Oldham Road and turns right for Tandle Hill Park. The players are put through a few stretching exercises before going on their run. To no one's surprise, the captain, Andy Thackeray, is soon out in front. Seems he is a natural athlete. Does this sort of thing for fun. Dave Bywater is particularly pleased to

5

see one or two of his YTS boys in the leading pack.
The trees provide welcome shade from the sun but it
is still too much for one youngster, who is gasping for
his inhaler. Another young lad is missing. Apparently he
was last seen back there somewhere, throwing up.

Docherty gives the players a short breather before
cajoling them into a series of hill climbs. One or two more
could do with inhalers now. They wind down with more
exercises and recover their sense of humour. One of the
backmarkers returns to inevitable wigging. He responds:
'If you'd been running properly you wouldn't have the
breath to say anything.' More derision from the others.

Docherty tells his players they'll resume at 1.30. In
the meantime, they can go off and have their steak and
chips. 'Is that on the club?' somebody asks. 'Thanks
very much.' They will have to draw sustenance from
Docherty's slight embarrassment. As they return to their
cars, the manager says: 'I'd like to be able to put on
some soup and fruit for them at lunchtime but I can't
do it, so they have to bring their own butties or go and
buy some.'

Docherty has a couple of trialists in the back of his
Ford Mondeo and, as he approaches Spotland, points
to the left saying: 'You can buy a butty there for 70p,
lads.'

Back in his office, he expresses himself content with
the first morning's work put in by the kids and 18
professionals. 'Especially considering the weather. It's
always hot, first day back. Guarantee it.'

A 19th professional, Dean Martin, phoned in to say he
couldn't make it. No, not a hangover. Also there has been
a call from a defender, Mark Wright – no, not that one
either – asking for a trial. The Doc says he will arrange

something. 'We get a lot of calls like this and you never know, one just might throw something up. We check them out and take it from there.'

Michael Mace, a director and a very useful man to have about the place because he happens to be an eminent surgeon, ambles in to the other Doc's office and says: 'Wake me up at the board meeting tonight if you should need me.'

'Thanks, I'll do that.'

Another caller is Steve Walmsley, the commercial manager. He reveals the £2,000 lottery prize has just been claimed by the 'scruffiest rag-bag you've ever seen and he wants it in cash. I told him, he can open a bank account now.' More irksome for the commercial department is the fact that they have had to pay out that fat cheque already. Walmsley also informs the manager he has a photographer from the *Rochdale Observer* coming round to take a picture of the new signing.

Before all that, Docherty is interviewed by the man who provides the club's newsline information, Mike Brookes.

'First of all, good morning Mick and good news this morning with a signing.'

'Yes, smashing, Mike, I'm delighted to announce that Ian Gray will join us. My chairman finalised the deal with Mr Stott, the Oldham chairman, and everything's gone through, so I'm very, very pleased. He looks a keeper of tremendous potential from what we saw in that three-month period. We've also got Chris Clarke, who had that horrendous injury last year – two very young and up-and-coming goalkeepers vying for one position. Most of last season we were begging, borrowing and stealing to get a goalkeeper.'

'Right Mick, the players have reported back now. What

7

sort of joys can they look forward to in terms of getting fit and blowing the cobwebs away?'

'Well, it will be quite a strenuous fortnight, Michael, because we have a game a week on Wednesday, against Bradford, which doesn't leave us an awful lot of time to get them match fit. They tend to come back sometimes a little overweight, one or two are prone to that. Others come back as if they've never been off and it's just a matter of getting everybody peaking at the right time.'

Docherty covers the Tandle Hill work and outlines his plans for sprints later in the week, plus ball work in the afternoons. 'You find some players don't enjoy running but when the ball's there they tend to forget they're tired and just get on with it.' Besides, it is quality, rather than quantity, he wants.

Walmsley returns. 'You wanted a word with Ian. He's gone down to get a sandwich but we'll get him in two minutes.'

'Is he wearing the training kit they're all wearing this morning?' Docherty asks.

'Yes.'

'That looks superb, that top, but what's it doing with Umbro on it?'

'That's the deal.'

'Do you want to have a word with Ian in the referee's room? It will be quieter in there.'

Sandwich dealt with, Gray is directed to the referee's room. Brookes resumes: 'What's made your mind up about coming back to Spotland?'

'First team football, basically. Didn't want to stay in the reserves,' Gray answers.

'Your first day at the club you've spent hill running. How did you enjoy that?'

'It's the easiest day I've had, actually, pre-season.'

'What are you looking forward to here at Rochdale?'

'I just want to establish myself, just get in the first team on a regular basis.'

'Not to forget Chris Clarke, we've now got two good young goalkeepers on the books. You will be able to help each other, I would imagine?'

'Yes, we can work together, but it should be a good battle.'

'Thanks very much, Ian Gray. That's Rochdale's new signing, Ian Gray, signed today from Oldham Athletic.'

Gray's next appointment is out on the pitch with the photographer, a squeaky-voiced photographer, which means he is the butt of some cruel mimicry. The grounds-man, merrily riding up and down the pitch on his mower, also has to take some ribbing. 'Hey, what's that green bit in the middle?' a player shouts over to him. The player has a point. The last time they were here, for that match in April, against Scarborough, it was a dustbowl with bumps.

To everyone's delight, the reserves have kept their place on this pitch and with it their place in the Pontins League. The club are not so lucky when it comes to a training ground. Without their own facility and unable to use Spotland for training, they wander like nomads, begging and borrowing pitches from local schools, clubs and the Council. This afternoon they have the use of a ground in Norden. After that, who knows?

Tuesday 18 July: a warm, muggy evening at Spotland. Dave Bywater, jovial and enthusiastic as ever, is at the main entrance, welcoming aspiring players and hopeful parents to a sort of open night. The youngsters are split into two age groups, despatched to the home or away dressing room accordingly and told: 'Don't touch anything or you'll get shot.'

Order, discipline and manners are part of the curriculum at the Centre of Excellence and any youngster who turns up for a match not wearing a tie is dropped. But then with the avuncular Bywater in command the regime is never likely to be intimidating. The parents are directed towards a suite in the main stand with the promise that the bar should be open soon.

Rochdale considers a thriving youth policy essential to its survival. It clearly saves money to produce your own and if you come up with a gem coveted by the big clubs you cash in. To those ends, the club has now established four junior teams and they are here tonight, en masse, for a photo call (they can buy their own copies, £1 each, black and white, mind, but every bit helps the coffers) and to watch a video on the dangers of drugs, accompanied by their parents. There is also a chance to catch up on arrangements for a 'fun day' at the ground. Every bit helps.

Bywater, who operates in tandem with the club's community officer, Keith Hicks, shepherds the youngsters, all now kitted out, to the stand to await their turn in front of the camera. Already on the pitch to join them is the manager. He presses a foot into the luxuriant turf and cannot disguise his frustration.

'We can't train on it, Hornets can't, that's the agreement, but I've suggested we could have it for an hour on Thursday morning, they could have it for an hour on Friday,' he says. 'They still won't let us. We were doing a bit of running up and down the cinders the other day and the players complained it was too hard, could they use the pitch. So I said okay, just the nearside, but somebody from Hornets came out and complained. Eventually I just told him where to go. Every now and then you've got to.'

As Docherty poses with his youngsters, Jimmy Robson, his trusted coach, knows the manager has first-team business on his mind. The first friendly, at home to Bradford City, is just 24 hours away; the opening League fixture, here against Cardiff, is a mere three and a half weeks from now.

'We've got to make a good start,' Robson says. 'We've not been able to bring in anybody really good and fresh, just the goalkeeper, so we need a good start to build up a bit of interest among the fans, get a bit of a spark and lift it. That's what he's anxious about.'

With his stick-on smile securely affixed, you would think Docherty hadn't a care in the world as he moves upstairs to address some 60 young players and their parents. Small and chirpy, one-liners ever on tap, he is the son of his father all right, a chip off the old Doc. This is his sales pitch. He tells the parents their offspring will get a chance here, that they should entrust their youngsters with Rochdale rather than a big club just as his father entrusted him with Burnley.

Next up is the chairman, who bemoans the fact that his manager has left him with nothing to say. 'He might not have had much of an education but my, can he talk!'

Both have more talking on the agenda this evening. Along the corridor, the Supporters' Club are holding their annual meeting, and Kilpatrick and Docherty are preparing themselves to be lined up and shot at. Doc would prefer to be put out of his misery but there are other matters to attend to, such as the election of officers and an explanation for the change of bus firms. The diehards are also introduced to someone who has offered his services to the club as a PR man, and are asked for any suggestions or observations. 'Good luck,' is the sole, sombre response from the floor.

The master of ceremonies is the chairman of the Supporters' Club, Frank Duffy, another undertaker-cum-orator with monologues to spare. Conscious Docherty has slid into the back of the room, Duffy proffers a kind of vote of confidence. 'All right, Doc's not everybody's choice, but he was left in an almost impossible situation at the end of last season, not knowing whether he was going to get the job, and a lot of people in his place would have said "stuff it". But he perserved and for that he deserves our support and encouragement.'

Still, though, the Doc must wait. It's the beer break next. Normally they meet down at the Ratcliffe Arms but they agreed to come upstairs as long as the club reduced the price of beer to that charged 'downstairs'. Kilpatrick, a more seasoned politician, suggests to Docherty that he should enjoy a pint.

Duffy persists with his performance into the interval, engaging Kilpatrick with a gag about an open day at the Chapel of Rest. Kilpatrick is anxious to rid Spotland of its funereal atmosphere, hence the flirtation with PR. 'I don't know what he can do but it's worth having a go. He's a bright lad, full of ideas and enthusiasm. The strange thing is that when we go away we have a good hard core of up to 500, who give terrific vocal support, yet at home it's totally different. They sit there, arms folded, with the glum expression that says "entertain me".'

While some of these supporters order another round, Docherty, having made overtures about another player, senses an appropriate moment to tackle the chairman: 'I've had a chat with him and I reckon we can get him for £350 a week.' Kilpatrick nods gently but his body language adds: 'Try and convince me a bit more.'

At last they are summoned to the meeting and Jimmy Robson is in on the PR act now, thanking the supporters for the donations used to buy sweaters for the youngsters at the Centre of Excellence. This audience, however, is not about to be softened up.

First question – in truth, more of a condemnation than a question – is for the chairman. The bone of contention is the restrictions on entry for home supporters at the opening League match, against Cardiff City, and the conclusion put to the chairman is that he does not care about the fans. Kilpatrick – a seasoned politician, remember – calmly refutes the claim, explaining that the club is tied by regulations. Having said that, the division of the spectator areas will be reviewed.

Kilpatrick shares some of the supporter's frustration over segregation rules, illustrating the 'madness of the situation' when they have to take the obligatory measures to accommodate 18 Barnet supporters. 'I told them we would have been better off sending them £10 a head not to come,' he says. The subject drags on beyond the endurance of one fan, who unceremoniously interjects: 'Can we talk about football?'

Seems a reasonable request and meets with general approval. Now Docherty is the target. What, for instance, does he see in a certain player who 'can't play at the back, can't play in midfield and can't play up front?' The fan goes on: 'From what I hear, his best position is on the back seat of a car on a Friday night!'

That's a tricky one, but Docherty is better prepared for

the dismay that he has not made more signings during the summer. He produces an A4 sheet of paper, its full length required to list the names of the players he inquired about but was unable to bring to Rochdale. David Speedie was retiring because of injury, the others were out of the club's financial range. Gary Bull, of Nottingham Forest, on about £1,500 a week and not interested in a loan deal; Andy Ritchie, also on well over £1,000 a week; and Stoke's Wayne Biggins, looking for a signing-on fee of £20,000-plus.

The Doc, therefore, is resigned to taking on the Third Division with the 'good' players he has. And then there's Paul Williams, a six foot three, 'mad' centre-forward. If he could get his finger out, says Docherty, 'he'd knock 'em over and kill 'em'. Alas, it doesn't always work like that.

The manager, now animated and impassioned, informs the gathering he wants success as much as they do. 'This is my livelihood,' he points out. 'If I don't do it I'm out the door.'

Then why doesn't the board come up with the money to pay the going rate?

'The club is in a deep, deep mess,' Kilpatrick announces. 'Two weeks ago we ran out of money. But something was sorted to pay out the wages. At the time we hadn't got the money to pay the wages, never mind buy players. We are penniless but it's not all doom and gloom. We have some players, we have a pitch to play on. We just don't have any money.'

CHAPTER TWO

Elusive Riches

The onset of matches, although only friendlies, brings a fresh urgency and a feeling of relief to Spotland. The line between essential training and tedium is fine and difficult to trace. Docherty has organised half a dozen games for his first-team squad, ample opportunity, he trusts, to test various permutations and strategies. Second Division Bradford City are sent packing back across the Pennines, beaten 4–0. Rochdale travel to Preston for a Marsden Lancashire Cup match and draw 2–2.

Dale's next engagement is on a training pitch and will be watched by a handful of people, but it is as eagerly anticipated as the League kick-off itself. The Doc's team are heading for the Cliff, Manchester United's Salford training headquarters, which will be off-limits to all but the chosen few because the opposition's line-up includes Eric Cantona, the Frenchman banned for eight months after practising his footwork on the chest of a Crystal Palace fan. If you are a Rochdale player the chances of your joining Le Roi for an afternoon are about as good as your prospects of receiving an invitation to a Buckingham Palace garden party, and immeasurably more appealing.

Alex Ferguson phoned up Docherty and said that he needed a game behind closed doors because of 'the Cantona situation' and would Rochdale be interested. Docherty readily accepted the challenge.

Rochdale are still dreaming deep into the 70-minute exercise. Dave Thompson's flicked header gives them the lead in 23 seconds and Paul Williams's lobbed volley from 40 yards beats Peter Schmeichel in the second half. To the amusement of the visitors, the volatile Danish goalkeeper and United's England central defender, Gary Pallister, have a heated set-to over responsibility for that second goal. Unfortunately for Dale, the embarrassment galvanises United and they win with three late goals. But no matter. Dale have rubbed shoulders with royalty today.

DOCHERTY
It was an opportunity for my players to play against players they might never come up against. Cantona is still sharp, very strong, with lovely awareness on the ball. He sees things other players just don't see. It's been a terrific experience for our players to meet that kind of quality. For the vast majority of the game we were leading and psychologically that's a tremendous boost. There's no doubt United's pride was pricked and they were at it after that, no messing. My players will be thinking if they can give them a game they can give anybody a game.

Giving Cantona a game, even behind closed doors, lands United in a touch of bother with the FA and although ultimately the matter would be swept away, the controversy again almost hounds the player out of the English game.

Rochdale lose less romantic encounters against Bolton

and Blackpool, and a sense of normality is restored. Just as well, perhaps. The League season is almost upon them. The result of a Football League Tribunal is not what they were looking for, yet better than it might have been. Dale wanted £30,000 for the transfer of Shaun Reid to Bury. The ruling awards Dale a minimum of £15,000, plus £5,000 after he has played 20 games for Bury and a further £5,000 after 40.

Injury forces the captain, full-back Andy Thackeray, out of the opening League match, at home to Cardiff, but Docherty declares himself 'pleased with the overall preparation'. He is less content watching his team squander a two-goal advantage against Cardiff and require a late third to scramble a draw. Entertaining it may be for the neutral, but who's neutral? The second week of the season is more productive: a 2–1 win in the home leg of a Coca-Cola Cup first round tie against Second Division York City and a 1–0 victory at Darlington in the League. Manager and players return to work buoyant. The mood runs through the office staff and among the directors. If the team can negotiate the return leg against York, they are in the money. The big clubs enter the next round – the prospect of big pay days, home and away.

Docherty is also optimistic about the potential of a new recruit. Paul Moulden, a schoolboy scoring sensation who ran out of goals in League football, has joined the club on a month's trial. He was one of those approached in the summer but his demands for £800 a week terminated discussions. 'Nobody's taken him on so his bargaining power has diminished drastically,' Doc says smugly. 'He's a free agent so I'm going to take a look at him. The goals have dried up for whatever reason, but he's only 27 and scoring is a bit like riding a bike – you never really lose that capacity to do it.'

Moulden will have to ride along with the reserves to start with, while Docherty sorts out the able-bodied for the trip to York.

DOCHERTY
We've got one or two injuries and a lot of it seems to be down to the weather. My physio says that because it's been so stiflingly hot the players can't get enough air in, the blood flow is not what it should be and consequently we're getting tweaks and strains.

Still, I'll settle for what we've done so far. It's fair to say I felt some trepidation. I've not been able to get the players I want and you're always a little concerned about what's going through the minds of the players and the punters. They want you to win but they are also waiting to shoot you down, so it's a no-win situation for a manager, really.

But it's been encouraging, especially considering the injuries. I'd like to think we could aim for the play-offs. Anything more would be a bonus. We've had to adapt and go for a sweeper system, and I'm glad to say that in the last two games it's worked quite well. The players have knuckled down. Gray is established. He's terrific. I'm fairly happy with midfield and central defence. But I need cover at full-back and I need another recognised striker and/or winger. Maybe Moulden will come into the picture there.

Apparently his midfield player, Jason Peake, has been the

subject of scouts' attention and a club like Rochdale does not discourage shoppers.

DOCHERTY
Peakey's doing terrific; Arsenal were here, Chelsea were here, Notts Forest were here. You don't want to lose players of that calibre when it's unlikely you will be able to replace them because the club needs any monies coming in. If you get a big fee you might have a proportion of it. That's why you're always on the look-out for one or two you might bring in.

It would mean an awful lot if we could go through in the Cup, particularly if we could draw one of the major clubs – your Tottenhams, your Newcastles, Arsenals, Man Us – simply for the financial reward. And as it's a two-legged affair, we would not only pick up a lot of money on their patch, we'd also have the wonderful situation of playing them in front of our own supporters. That would be a major boost for a club like ours. Say we got United, you're looking at something in the region of £150,000. It can take you all winter to bring in money like that. And that's why the Cup is so important.

But as a manager there's something else to look forward to, something I've always wanted – to pit my wits against one of the Premier League managers. I've been here four and a half years, originally as assistant manager, doing all the coaching. I've always been philosophical because I know if I'm doing the job well and the club's successful then the likelihood is that someone will come in and get me anyway. I don't have set goals and I was never thinking I'd have Dave Sutton's job here. I've always been loyal and Dave was relaxed because he knew I wasn't after his job. I was there to protect him, work with him and for him.

When Dave lost his job I took what was available to me – the job on a temporary basis. There was a lot of debate about whether I should get it and that was hard to a degree. I've been a footballer all my life and I knew what was required. I realised I had to do the job to the best of my ability so that even if someone else came in they might feel I deserved to be kept on. I had to safeguard my present job, and that's why you have to carry on regardless.

Eventually I got the job of manager, but I haven't got a contract. I've never had a contract at this club. In the first two years I used to phone the chairman constantly because I think all of us want a little bit of security, but it's something that in the past they've been bitten by. They've had to sack people for whatever reason and of course they've then had to pay out compensation so they felt it was in their best interests not to give me a contract. I could see their point of view. I wasn't happy with it, still not happy with it, but you get on with it. [They get accustomed to getting on with it at this end of the football spectrum.]

Finances govern what you can and can't do. For example, we'll have about eight long trips this season, yet only perhaps three of them – Plymouth, Exeter and Gillingham – will be overnight trips. Torquay is an evening kick-off, so we'll leave on the morning of the match and get back in the early hours of the following morning. That's the kind of area where they pull in the purse strings. Sometimes for a local trip such as Bury, we don't get a coach because we can save a couple of hundred pounds. The players just meet up at Bury's ground.

Every opportunity they can, they save what they can. I know the score. It's second nature to me now. I just accept it for what it is. We're not alone. There'll be other clubs who are probably worse off than us. I was astonished to hear Middlesbrough fly to a lot of matches, but if they can afford it there's no doubt it's the right way. They are priming their players and the players must realise the club are doing everything in their power to smooth the way for a good performance from them. They've no excuses and believe me, players do look for excuses. I mustn't give my players the impression they've got an excuse. I've got to be optimistic.

Back to the stick-on smile. Does Dad have any other advice?

DOCHERTY
He never really gets involved. When I was a kid he sent me to Burnley when I could have gone to the likes of Liverpool, Arsenal or Tottenham, and I'm grateful for that, as I told the kids the other night. I broke through at 17 years and 11 months and now at our club we have Dave Bayliss a first-year pro, 18 years of age, and he's played the last two games in the first team and done really well. My dad's always there if I want advice and I wouldn't think twice about going and asking him, but he never offers it now.

Being the son of a famous father can be a dubious privilege. Being the son of Tommy Docherty can be a decided disadvantage.

DOCHERTY
I dare say it's been a help *and* a hindrance. I know I've lost jobs in the past just because of my name. 'If he's anything like his dad . . .', you know, that kind of thing, which I think is very fickle. One was Tranmere, as manager before the John King era. I have to be careful what I say about the other, to be honest. There's no love lost between me and that club, a club I played for. To lose jobs like that because of that was a bit galling at the time, but I dare say it's got me in jobs as well, so you take the rough with the smooth.

Docherty, who also played for Manchester City and Sunderland, has bittersweet recollections of confronting the Manchester United side managed by his father. Football folk love to reminisce and Mick Docherty is no exception.

DOCHERTY
My debut for City was at Old Trafford and of course there was a big build-up in the Press: Doc v Doc, father and son, all that sort of thing. Come the day, I'm marking Gordon Hill, a terrific winger, and I absolutely froze. My legs were just leaden. Couldn't move. We lost 2–0. When I was with Burnley we had some tremendous battles with Leeds. Talk about intimidatory tactics. Leeds were something else.

We'd put five past them on our ground and at the end of the match none of their players would shake hands with us. Billy Bremner just said they'd be ready for us at their place.

In those days teams didn't go out for the kick-off together, they went out individually, but as we came out of our dressing room at Elland Road, Bremner was standing in the corridor bouncing a ball. Suddenly, the Leeds players appeared and started filing out alongside us. 'What's all this about,' we wondered. One player was right at the back and as we set off down the tunnel he whacked Taffy [Leighton James] on the back of the head. Taffy was terrified after that. Couldn't do a thing. They put six past us. Nice team, that Leeds.

The Doc has a slight headache with his list of injuries and briefs Michael Mace on the various problems. He'll catch up with his admin in the afternoon, then go home, sleep on his selection options and dream of rich pickings.

It promises to be another evening of erratic blood flow. The hot weather shows no signs of abating and club officials mill around the main entrance with jackets flung over shoulders. One man conspicuous by his absence is David Kilpatrick. 'The chairman's not coming,' Mace informs Docherty. 'He says he's a jinx.'

Mace also has some information for a lady emerging from the office: 'You won't be seeing me in the boardroom tonight. I don't get on with them there. They're not the gentlemen they used to be.'

This enigmatic pronouncement is swiftly followed by more expressions of dissatisfaction. The bus waiting to take the team on their treasure hunt across the Pennines is not good enough, he tells Docherty. Docherty agrees. Besides, where is the Rochdale AFC sign? They may be poor, but they have standards. Where's their usual bus? The one Blackburn Rovers use.

At 4.32 their sub-standard bus (the one-level type as opposed to the trendy split-level job) pulls away from Spotland, accompanied by more drones of complaint. They are unhappy about the *Manchester Evening News* report of their last match. 'I don't read the papers anyway,' a voice claims. Docherty sits back with a copy of the *Daily Telegraph*.

Steve Walmsley and Jimmy Robson turn their attention to tea – barm cakes. Docherty has one and then disappears into the back, returning with coffees. 'Who's for sugar?' By now a video is running: last night's Leeds v Liverpool match. Most want another look at Tony Yeboah's volley. Docherty would like a first look at it. 'Haven't got Sky,' he says.

We climb Saddleworth Moor and drop into West Yorkshire. How many times some of them must have followed this M62 trail. 'I helped build it,' Robson reveals.

Helped build it?

'Aye,' returns the gentle North-East voice. 'I was freed by Barnsley and got a job labouring. I'm an electrician by trade but I was labouring on here for a month. Long hours, Saturday and Sunday, too. Good money, though. Then I got fixed up at Bury. Before the motorways, all journeys were long. Birmingham and Villa were overnights from Burnley. We used to go to London on the train and stay overnight. We'd go to Bow Street Magistrates, for a laugh, you know. Cheaper than the pictures.'

This journey along the M62 is interrupted to pick up a

player at Hartshead Services. Another two players from this side of the hills have been delayed in traffic and relay the message they will drive straight to York. The stop has given Walmsley the chance to bring on more supplies: chocolate and cans of fizzy drink.

Back on the road Peakey, who is evidently the video kid, forward winds Andy Gray's half-time subbuteo analysis. 'Way over the top,' comes the chorus. There is a dissenting voice when Yeboah's goal is shown. 'It was a fluke, that.' Others just dream of flukes.

Docherty is more pragmatic and pores over Robson's report on tonight's opponents. The notes on York's individual and collective strengths and weaknesses will influence his formation and strategy.

The first sighting of York Minster is Docherty's signal to hand out complimentary tickets to players and officials. This city, always alluring, is more enchanting than ever this balmy evening.

At 6.19, Rochdale's team coach reverses through the gates to York City's Bootham Crescent ground. They are a little earlier than Docherty would have preferred for the 7.45 kick-off. 'Ideally you want to be at the ground an hour before the match, but you have to leave yourselves a bit of a margin, just in case.' He would gladly forfeit this next hour or more of his life, fretting and fidgeting as he does. He smiles and speaks to all-comers, but he is tense, nervously shuffling between the pitch and the dressing room. 'This is the worst bit,' he says. 'You just want to get on with it.'

Docherty, Robson and Walmsley are now wearing smart, light green, checked jackets. 'We try to look the part,' the manager says. 'Besides, they're light and cheap.' Robson admits his casual shoes may not be everybody's idea of looking the part, but explains: 'They're my lucky ones. They've worked so far.' Most football people are superstitious. 'I have lucky socks and underpants,' Docherty confirms.

The players jog out for a loosener in their black and green change strip and training tops. 'Look good, don't they?' Doc says. 'Again, it's having pride in your appearance. When we came here four and a half years ago they were a Rag, Tag and Bobtail outfit, all sorts of bits and pieces.'

The pitch also looks good but Docherty is not so sure. 'The grass is a bit too long for my liking.'

He scuttles back inside, leaving Robson out on the pitch, surveying the players. You cannot help wondering whether these young men have any idea of what their quiet, modest coach achieved as a player. 'I doubt it,' he says, smiling and shuffling uneasily on those trusted old shoes. 'I don't really talk about it, not unless they ask.'

Docherty breezes back, clutching York's teamsheet, and consults Robson. They reckon they know what to expect and the manager returns to the dressing room, followed by his players.

'He prefers to keep busy,' Robson observes. 'He organises the kit as well, you know. Gets it cleaned at the Infirmary laundry.'

Ten minutes before kick-off, the players are called to order and sit for their final instructions from the manager. He sways back and forth assuring them: 'Set yourselves a platform. Take your time. We can afford that. Take the sting out of them for the first 15–20 minutes and it can be yours – and so can a plum tie.'

'And an overnight?' a player asks.

'It might be United.'

'Still like an overnight.'

'If we get a plum, you can have your overnight no matter where we are.'

A crescendo of 'good luck' wishes and cries of 'we can do it' greets the referee's bell, which calls them to action. Handshakes and backslaps all round, and then the distinctive patter of studs on hard floor fades down the corridor. Docherty, never idle for a moment, trawls sweatshirts scattered around the dressing room, counts them back into the skip and discovers one in a player's bag. 'Look at that. Typical.'

He is more appreciative of the green and black replica shirts in profusion behind one of the goals. 'We must have about 200 fans here,' he says, settling on the bench with the physio, John Dawson, to his left and the substitutes to his right. He's not settled for long. Moments into the match he is animated, demanding: 'Tight, tight . . . stay with the runners.'

The intensity of the contest on the pitch is seemingly matched by that on the benches. Docherty and Dawson shout; Alan Little and his aides shout louder; Docherty and Dawson shout louder still. Barely two minutes into the game the shouts from Docherty and Dawson become groans. A raid down the left by York, the ball in, goal. The early bombardment they were warned about has found them wanting and now the aggregate scores are level. Docherty is momentarily dumbstruck. He soon recovers his voice, urging his centre-forward, that giant of a man, Paul Williams, to 'get up, get up'. Dawson shakes his head in dismay. 'He's not won a ball. He never jumps his height.'

For the consumption of the bench only, Docherty has equally critical remarks, but his yells to the players are always positive, intended to lift rather than deflate. He even has a kind word for everybody's whipping boy when a tight decision goes Rochdale's way: 'Good positioning, referee.'

A wag just behind the bench is less impressed with Docherty's antics. 'You're up and down more than Punch and Judy,' he protests. 'Put some superglue on his arse.'

Half-time and still 1–0 on the night. The dressing room is distinctly quieter than when they left it, but voices are raised in the far corner. Peake, standing alongside the much taller Williams, says: 'You've been going on at me for a month, and then look what you do.'

Williams counters but gleans little sympathy from his colleagues and Docherty takes over.

'I told you before the match you'd be under pressure,' he says. 'It will be the same in the second half. Midfielders in particular, think about the eight and four. Once or twice they've had little changeovers. Got to be aware of that . . . Need to be sharper and more aggressive on the ball . . . You've got to look to play it. Don't mind you looking for the big man in certain areas of the field, but not all the time. It's the same with the ball over the top for Whitey and Thommo . . . Two full-backs doing okay. Once you were unlucky, Kevin. You were a bit too much square of the ball but I don't mind that, son . . . Other than that I'm quite happy with it. Work rate's good. You've got back in the game. Thommo's got wonderful crosses in. We just need bodies in the box.'

The players give themselves another gee-up. 'We'll do it,' they concur, and go back to work.

Even superglue would not contain Docherty four minutes into the second half. York score again and he pummels the air with his fist and expletives. This is where a manager has to think on his feet – or his backside. The Doc's remedy is to dispense with the sweeper and take the game to the Second Division side. The transformation is spectacular. Low ball in, own goal; 3–3 on aggregate. Docherty is airborne.

Both benches seem on the verge of apoplexy and a patronising voice from the gallery contends: 'It's only a game.'

Are you sure?

Rochdale are in the ascendancy and Docherty is kicking every ball, sliding into every tackle. 'We're going to win this, we're going to win this,' Dawson murmurs.

The York bench fear he's right. 'We're dead,' someone solemnly declares.

But for the heroics of their goalkeeper, they would be. He makes two particularly splendid saves from Steve Whitehall. Four minutes from the end of normal time, however, he is at the mercy of Williams. Inside the six-yard box, routine header, he must score, must win the tie. He heads over. Disbelief, gut-wrenching disappointment. No one says as much, but on the bench they know that could have cost them the tie.

Extra time deepens their suspicions. An injury to central defender Paul Butler, a pivotal figure in this team, ruins their powers of resistance. Ian Gray ultimately succumbs. 'That's the keeper's every time,' Docherty confidently states as the ball loops into Gray's territory. It isn't this time. He fumbles and is punished. Twice he has been at fault now and York romp on to a 5–1 win, 6–3 overall. It is a harsh scoreline, but then it is a harsh game, and Rochdale have been here before. The players flop onto the benches. Some curse their fate. Others are silent. All are deflated.

Docherty addresses them: 'Right with the attitude, but you've got to look at yourselves with two goals tonight. You can't afford to make mistakes, you know that. The overall performance I was quite pleased with, particularly your second half, but for half an hour you were absolutely taken. You've just got to pick yourselves up and start again. You've got an important League game on Saturday and we've got to get back on track and get three points.

'You've got to face the fact that we've got to chop and change. I changed it when the second one went in because I felt we had to have a go at them. Get up and get three points at the weekend and we'll be nice and happy again. Have a nice rest tomorrow. Anyone with injuries see John tonight before you go. It's quarter past ten, we'll call it quarter past eleven on the bus and then we'll get away. Come on, get your heads up.'

Docherty leaves them to shower, change and replay the match over a drink in the players' bar. He heads for the boardroom but is intercepted by Mike Brookes and the *Rochdale Observer*'s man, Les Barlow. Docherty effortlessly switches on.

'The scoreline belies how well we played, particularly in the second half,' he tells them. 'When they got the second goal – which I felt Ian Gray was to blame for as he should have come and claimed it – we needed to change it, went to a flat back four and for half an hour I thought we played particularly well. Steve Whitehall has had a great header saved, Paul Williams should have scored with a header from virtually underneath the bar . . . But delighted with their application, showed a lot of resolve and character . . . I felt over the 90 minutes we deserved to win the tie.'

'Injuries?'

'It looks like Butler will be out, Shaw will be out, Thompstone will be out, Valentine, too, so I'm going to have to jig about. Obviously we need to shore up one or two things at the back but when you're chopping and changing as we're having to it makes it a little bit unsettling for the team as a whole. I'm going to look at the reserve game against Darlington on Thursday and see what I can take from that.'

That regular chore tended to, Docherty makes it to the boardroom and has a drink and chat with his opposite number, Alan Little, brother of more famous Brian, Aston Villa's manager. Elsewhere in the room Graham Morris is engaged in conversation with York's chairman, Douglas Craig, a seemingly hospitable Scot, but then when you have made it to the hat with the big boys you can well afford the largesse. Pity the beer is warm.

Football's boardrooms have a culture all of their own, far removed from the stands and the dressing rooms. This is more of a gentleman's club. And a club for wives of gentlemen. The groups of directors and wives rotate, bumping into each other at least twice a season if they are in the same division. Every meeting is like a reunion, and mostly they talk about money, who they can sell (Craig reckons their 'keeper is worth a bit) and what's coming through the gate.

Morris is studying a slip of paper bearing details of the attendance and receipts: 2,130 spectators, a little under £12,500. 'That includes VAT and out of that they've got to pay the match officials and meet the other usual costs. We'll get out of it, I suppose, 3½ to 4 grand. Had we gone through to the next round, we would have been looking at a minimum of 50 grand. That's what it's cost us.'

Since women are not allowed on the team coach, Morris and his wife have driven to the match and are still talking to their host as Docherty and the rest climb back on the coach for the return to Rochdale. The manager reaches for his stick-on smile and suggests: 'When the chairman sees the result he'll go berserk.'

But how was it for you, Doc?

DOCHERTY
The things you've seen tonight are the things you have to learn to live with as a manager. No disrespect to our players, but if they were more sure of themselves, more aware of their responsibilities, these things wouldn't happen. Consequently, that's why they're playing in the Third Division. But they're a great set of lads, I thoroughly enjoy working with them, they give me their all and I can ask for no more than that. There's a great spirit.

If you had a very good side, a classy side such as Man United – teams of that ilk – you know you are going to be there or thereabouts at the end of the season and when they go 2–0 or 3–0 up, the manager can just sit back and enjoy a cigar because he knows there's no way they are going to surrender that lead. At my level that's not the case. We can be 2–0 or 3–0 up and not be sure of the outcome, so you can never completely relax. You can't really enjoy it until the final whistle.

The final whistle brought no relief this evening and, for all the spirit he vaunts, he cannot ignore the friction between

Williams and some of the other players. Williams's contract runs until the end of the season and Docherty's attempt to pay him off after last season was blocked by the board. Williams wanted his £25,000, Docherty offered £10,000, they agreed £17,000, but the board said 'No'. Williams told his manager: 'I'll prove you wrong.'

Docherty, still awaiting that proof, admits: 'I daren't play him at home because the crowd go mad. They can't stand him. It's a situation we've got to sort out.' Wider problems were brought home to him again in that post-match chat with his opposite number. 'It was interesting to hear Alan Little does similar things to us in training – shadow play, he repeats set-pieces, both for and against, pattern play, how to get forward, etc. I do all that. The only thing is he's got a training ground and he can also train on his first-team pitch. I can do neither. You just have to get on with it, not feel sorry for yourselves, and our lads don't. I'm not disillusioned, never have been.'

The chances are, he will be digesting the game in general and this match in particular into the early hours. 'Once we get back I'll drive home, just grab a bit of supper, a Chinese unless I've got something in. I can't eat for two or three hours after a match. I'll have a couple of beers and won't really get to sleep until two or three in the morning because I'll be thinking over the game. I have a habit of thinking of things in the middle of the night and having to write them down.'

The Chinese and beers will have to wait a while longer. The bus arrives back at Spotland at five minutes past midnight and Doc supervises the unloading of the skips. He also has a few more words with Robson about the reserve team to play at Darlington on Thursday. 'I'll go up in my car,' the manager says.

An evening that started with dreams of Manchester United and riches ends with the logistics of a reserve game at Darlington. And who do York draw in the next round of the Coca-Cola Cup? United, of course.

CHAPTER THREE

Long Bad Tuesday

Rochdale's players dutifully have their heads up for the home match against Hartlepool and, despite the enforced changes, they register an emphatic 4–0 win, 18-year-old Jamie Taylor claiming a hat trick. Optimism filters through the club again. Dale are third. Surely they are on for another three points at Torquay – who are bottom and without a point – which would set up a top-of-the-table clash with Northampton at Spotland next Saturday, because they are bound to win. All so blissfully straightforward, isn't it, this mind game of football?

The Grand Plan occupies most of the passengers climbing on board the coach for the trip to Devon. Even the coach fits the bill this time. It's the one Blackburn Rovers use. A steady drizzle has little prospect of permeating Docherty's enthusiasm. He is busy, as usual, loading the kit. 'Come on, Jamie, help me with the skips. Keep your feet on the ground.'

He recruits another, unsuspecting player: 'You can help as well, since you're laughing.'

There are plenty of smiles after Saturday's result. The

chairman is here, too, the jinx theory patently discounted after York. He and Walmsley are marvelling at Wigan Rugby League team's latest wondrous display. Another discussion revolves around players in the lower divisions of the Endsleigh League and the Conference, updates on old sparring partners at Scunthorpe and Altrincham – names most out there will never have heard of.

The conversation becomes focused on one topic when someone mentions Manchester United's victory at Blackburn the previous night. 'They played like you, Peakey,' Kilpatrick says. 'Mind you, Williams is better than Sutton at the moment.'

'Steady on, chairman,' Walmsley cautions. Williams is not on this trip.

At eleven o'clock, the scheduled departure time, there's still no sign of Dean Martin, so Kilpatrick steps out of the coach for a cigarette. 'Not allowed to smoke on there,' he mutters, ruefully, although he neither expects nor receives sympathy.

Martin screeches to a halt in the car park and jumps aboard at 11.05 to chants of 'fine, fine, fine' from his team-mates.

'Yes,' Docherty affirms, 'twenty quid on match days.'

'I'm just glad to be here,' Martin dolefully responds. 'Traffic on the motorway's terrible.'

The instant the coach turns a wheel Peake is feeding a tape into the video recorder. Now, Docherty, too, can enjoy United's passing exhibition at Ewood Park.

The chairman manages another quick drag as the coach pulls off the M6 into Knutsford Services to pick up a batch of players domiciled between Manchester and Merseyside. Satisfied with the intake of nicotine and personnel, Kilpatrick bids the driver to venture on: 'We've got enough now. If we can't beat them with this lot it's a bad job.'

In common with most travelling clubs, Rochdale have very clearly understood demarcation lines on the coach. Officials sit at the front, players from the back, and between them tends to be a no-go area. The chairman, now condemned to a lengthy no smoking ordeal, attempts some paper work but soon gives up in despair. This is a British motorway, chairman. He and Docherty find more satisfaction in the *Evening News* report on Dale's last match.

Unsurprisingly, Docherty has named Taylor for tonight's match. 'He's a kid who's come through the ranks, YTS last year. We signed him because other clubs were sniffing around. That's four in four games he's got. I took him off after he scored his third goal so he could get an ovation all to himself, and he did. Brought Williams on and they booed him. If he can't get the message now . . . I've left him at home today. He doesn't like it but I don't care. It's the end product that matters to me. Valentine's got to have a cartilage operation, which is a bit of a blow.'

So is the traffic approaching Birmingham, but then isn't it always? The solution is a detour through Wolverhampton. By now Blackburn and United have given way to *Only Fools and Horses*, the one where they go on a coach trip to the seaside, stop on the way at a pub and see their transport blown up. The Rochdale team bus stops at a service area on the M5 – 'just 10 minutes, to stretch the legs, lads' – and the break passes without serious incident.

The chairman, however, has some serious smoking to catch up on. And some serious thinking. 'Sod's Law, York getting United, wasn't it? Would have done us nicely, that. Taken all the pressure off.'

Mace interjects: 'We wouldn't have got United. It doesn't work like that. We would have had Leicester.'

Still Sod's Law.

Kilpatrick goes on: 'Had a young chap round doing a piece for that Q-something or other magazine, wanted to know "what's it like living in the shadow of Man United?" I lost my rag a bit. "What's United got to do with us?" I said. "If that's the best you can ask me forget it. Do your article and don't ask me about United." He was a bit upset but I'm sick of being asked about United. Ask the other 90 clubs what it's like – they're all in the shadow of United. United have the money and good luck to them. I don't envy them.

'An analogy I use is that a friend of mine has a family hotel in Rochdale, very well run, fine. But he's not Rocco Forte. There's no comparison. We run Rochdale Football Club to the best of our ability. If people from Rochdale go off and support United and complain about the cost, I've no sympathy for them.'

Legs – and lungs – stretched, and drivers changed, the players and officials settle down for the next part of the show, *Blackadder*. 'I like this,' Kilpatrick says. The weather and scenery down this end of the country are to the liking of everyone aboard. The coach has turned off the M5, along a fiendishly tight, twisting lane towards Honiton. Into the village of Weston and another world. 'Ducks on loose, keep dogs on lead,' instructs a sign.

Another squeeze through a couple of gates and Rochdale's players are let loose at the Deer Park Hotel, a delightful watering hole Burnley recommended to

Docherty. The players have scrambled eggs and beans on toast. The officials, in another room, eat steak and chips, washed down with iced water. The club have some of their occasional overnight stops here. 'They do us a very good deal,' Docherty says.

That delay in the West Midlands squeezed the team for time and after three-quarters of an hour the bus is again negotiating those two gates, then turning right towards Exeter and Torbay. 'English Riviera' is the somewhat presumptious roadside proclamation that indicates the team are almost at journey's end. Doesn't look too much like Juan-les-Pins in Torquay United's neighbourhood, but in fairness the ground is called Plainmoor. After 296 miles, Rochdale are relieved just to be here.

Kick-off is little more than an hour away, which suits Docherty better than last week, and he is into his pre-match rituals again. Jimmy Robson has missed this trip because of reserve and youth team commitments, leaving John Dawson to take some of the chores off the manager's shoulders. Dawson sets up his medical equipment and reckons he has the means to cope with just about any injury or mishap. 'Players try to catch me out, but they can't.'

Some of the players take a shower to flush the mileage from their bodies. 'That's good, lads,' the boss approves. He has private words of encouragement and guidance for Taylor, a slip of a lad who doesn't even look 18.

Others flick through the programme and discover 'one of the linesmen is a woman'. Most resist sexist comment but John Deary cannot. 'She should be at home, in the kitchen, where women belong,' he feels compelled to say, albeit with a grin rippling across his face.

The clock runs down: time for the final team talk.

'Mentally you've got yourselves tuned and got yourselves right, and if you go out there and approach the game in the right manner and you're attacking and you're sharp and you're at it, you will get that first goal and you'll go home with the game ... Attack everything, man to man. Don't give any silly free-kicks away. Don't sell yourselves. Deano, you get 'em out, son.'

Docherty pauses, goes on a short prowl, returns to the centre of the dressing room, checks his watch and continues. 'You've got three minutes and you're out. Come on, final preparations. I don't want a repetition of York, two minutes. You make sure we get tight on people and don't be giving away any silly free-kicks, either. Don't let me waste my breath on you. Make yourselves hard to beat, boys ... Come on, get your shirts tucked in. I want you looking the part. You look the part, you play the part ... Don't give them chances to get in the box, just think about that ... There it is, boys, get out there. Good luck.'

The players come in with their own soundbites of faith and hope, like disciples at an evangelical rally. They jump to their feet and march on as purposefully and worthily as Christian soliders.

Docherty and Dawson crouch into the dugout, one of those traditional little concrete chambers that discourage managers from leaping to their feet. The aforementioned linesperson, Wendy Toms, is patrolling the far side of the pitch and Docherty has a message for the official running the near line: 'Hey, lino, your legs aren't as nice as the other one's.'

Five minutes into the match, his mood has changed. Don O'Riordan, Torquay's wily old pro and aspiring young boss, is running the show from deep and Rochdale are showing no signs of getting to grips with him. 'Go four,' Docherty screams to his defence, releasing Martin to counter O'Riordan.

Screams for a penalty are contemptuously ignored by the referee, Roger Gifford. (Yes, *that* Roger Gifford. There were rumours he had been seen in these parts being wheeled along the front with a tartan blanket across his legs. But here he is, still whistling.)

'Put him under pressure . . . Keep knocking them balls, Peakey . . . One behind you, But . . . Time, Buttie, time.' The stream of instructions is endless.

The Doc is rendered speechless after 32 minutes, however. His left-back, Kevin Formby, aims a kick at an opponent virtually in front of the dugout and the red card is inevitable.

Docherty is content to reach the sanctuary of the dressing room at half-time with the match still scoreless. Between the expletives, he says: 'You've got problems. One, the way you're playing; two, you're down to 10 men. The longer you stay in the game at 0–0, the more opportunities are going to arise for you. You can only play one way. You've got to condition your minds now and do exactly the same as them . . . If the opportunity doesn't arrive in the second half I might change it. If I pull people off it's for a particular reason . . . Just think about the cover for your two centre-halves. The lesser of two evils is the ball going to the winger and then you've just got to deal with it as best you can.

'It's a difficult game for everybody. You've got to be concentrating all the time. Make sure you don't lose. You've got to graft. Your competitive edge has got to be right on. Don't succumb to them playing against you, match it tooth and nail. If you do that, I'm telling you now, you'll come out with a result. Take your time. If you can catch them out, then do it . . . In a situation like this, you play percentage football. Take no chance. Don't give them the chance to have a pop at you on the edge of the box. Stand up and squeeze the ball from deep.'

He paces the small, spartan room, head bowed in thought. The tone of his delivery is less harsh as he again takes up his central position and gestures one or two of his restless charges back to attention.

DOCHERTY
Sit down a sec, I'll just tell you a little story, going back to my own career. Playing for Sunderland, we had our two full-backs sent off against Burnley, of all teams. Nine men at half-time we had, and ended up beating them 2–1 simply because we wanted it so bad, 'cos we were angry at the situation, we were angry at our team-mates, we were angry at the referee and everything else that was going on.

Now if you're like that, if you're up for that, you take that anger out, if it's conditioned anger, take it into the right areas of the field, and I'll tell you what, you can come out with not only a point but a win. It depends how badly you all want it. I'm not bothered about the result. Yes, I want to win, but if you give your all, hook, line and sinker, you can win the game because they're not that clever. Let's think about it.

So that's what it was like backstage at the Alamo . . .

Seven minutes into the second half, O'Riordan crosses from the right and as his left-back leaps into the ball's flightpath Docherty concedes the worst. 'Goal,' he says.

Goal it is. Only Torquay's second in four matches. It is enough to stir the locals – the seagulls as well as the punters.

Docherty ponders for a few minutes and is stirred into activity. He takes off Martin and Taylor, who is not so effective tonight. 'Got to try something different, lads,' he explains, almost apologetically.

Rochdale are not merely containing but forcing. With a little over 10 minutes left Docherty decides to go for broke. He pulls off Bayliss and plays three at the back. 'We might lose it 2–0 but what the hell. Got to have a go.'

A header is just wide, a shot is scrambled away. Behind the goal, Dale's loyal 135, defiantly displaying a huge blue and white banner, play their vociferous part. Alas, to no avail. An equaliser eludes them. Docherty and his players demonstrate their appreciation to the supporters and retreat to their bunker beneath the stand.

The yells of jubilation from the home dressing room convey the importance of a team's first points and compound the misery behind the visitors' door. Docherty does not have to call them to order. They slump in a row before him, some wearily tugging at their bootlaces, some swigging from bottles of water, others motionless, emotionally ravaged, staring at their feet. In the corner of this stark, soulless cell, to the manager's left, sits Formby. Long since showered and changed, he wears his sense of guilt like a sack cloth.

'Tell you what,' Docherty begins, looking straight ahead, 'as a manager, coach or anybody, I couldn't ask any more of you. Absolutely different class. Your attitude, your effort, your application. At the end of the day you had them crapping themselves with ten men.

We could have snatched it right at the death. Thommo could have scored, Whitey could have scored. I'm pleased to be associated with you because if you do that we've got a chance, and you know that yourselves. Don't get disillusioned or downhearted because at the end of the day he knows it and I know it – you cost us, Kevin.'

Docherty wheels to his left and points an accusing finger at the forlorn figure in the corner. Formby nods in contrite acknowledgement, avoiding eye contact with his manager and his team-mates.

'A rash decision on your part,' the judgement continues. 'You cost us. You might think it's unfair to put the blame on you, Kevin, but that's the way it is.'

Docherty switches his attention to Bayliss. 'Sometimes we've got to change it for a reason. There's nothing in that, David. Anyway, that was terrific. Right now it's 9.40. Ten past, that gives you half an hour. Ten past ten on the bus.'

Torquay's new stand, behind the goal to the left, houses the boardroom and the long winding walk is worth the effort. These are renowned hosts and the fare on offer is doubtless intended to make their guests feel at home: Lancashire hot pot and curry. Rochdale's officials are digesting the results on teletext. Northampton have lost to Hartlepool, the team third from bottom before tonight.

'How did they manage that?' asks Kilpatrick.

'Like we did,' replies a colleague.

So much for the top-of-the-table clash. This is the scenario they were all dreading: climbing on to the bus for the seemingly endless trek home after a defeat. A couple of miles down the road, the Doc prescribes something to ease the pain. 'Pull up just here, will you?'

he implores the driver. 'Come on lads, I'll buy you a drink.'

They troop across the road – players in tracksuits, officials in jackets, collars and ties – to the comforting embrace of a hostelry. It will, however, take more than a lager to comfort the chairman. 'Even a point would have helped Saturday's gate,' he sighs. 'Now they'll look at the score, a 1–0 defeat, and say "Rochdale's back to normal".'

Kilpatrick takes his drink to another table for a tête-à-tête with Docherty, leaving the obvious question trailing in his cigarette smoke: Why do it? What do these successful, professional men get out of the game when they are constantly stifled by a melancholic shroud? 'Well, not for money,' Mace says. 'They may be in it for the money in the Premier League. This club probably wouldn't exist but for the likes of David Kilpatrick and Graham Morris. We're in it, I suppose, for the fun.'

Mace's notion of fun is famously bizarre and mischievous. 'Did you know,' he challenges, 'that the memory span of a fish is eight seconds?'

Well, actually, no.

Mace explains, in an accent that would probably be deemed posh for Rochdale, that his boycott of the York boardroom followed an incident during a match last season, when he and the equally unceremonious Walmsley exchanged verbal brickbats with the natives and the home club reacted by sending a pompous letter of complaint to the League.

Mace's black humour was wasted on the safety inspector who sat next to him at a home match and who, glancing up at a plane on its way into Manchester Airport, asked what the director would do if a plane crash-landed on the pitch. 'That would depend on the score,' the good doctor replied, drily. 'If we were winning, we'd carry on playing around the plane.'

The man from the grey palace was apparently not amused.

A drink and a chat with the chairman appear to have fortified Docherty's humour. Dropping off for a pint like that is important.

DOCHERTY

It's team spirit. They might feel they've let you down, they've lost the game, and sometimes it's better to stop for a pint after losing than it is when you've won. A lot of managers might not see it like that but I do.

It's the same if we're away on an overnight. I'm happy for the players to have a half pint, or two halves, but not pints, the night before a game. If you forbid them a drink they may go behind your back. It's a case of treating them as men, as responsible pros, the way I preferred to be treated when I was a player. You get the player's respect and he says 'the gaffer'll do for me'.

[Handling directors may be a different matter.] I've discussed with the chairman the performance and the difficulties of the situation due to the sending off. He's delighted with the performance of the players but disappointed with one or two aspects. They're all entitled to their opinions, but they are not professional men in terms of football and I would never presume to tell them how to run their businesses. Consequently, I would like to think they would give me the same consideration.

But fair dos to David Kilpatrick. He has an opinion and as chairman of a football club he's entitled to such, and he said to me he thought the players gave me everything, which they did. What pleased me more than anything else was that he felt the club was going forward and that is the most encouraging thing from my short span of time with the football club. Even in defeat, I felt good.

I thought that up to Formby being sent off we were holding our own. It's debatable whether it cost us the game but in my experience in football, which has been a long time, it almost certainly was a large percentage of the reason for our defeat. He will be punished in accordance with the disciplinary code of the football club, which is 25 per cent of his wages. If I had my way it would be a week's wages, but unfortunately we can't do that.

The problem now is that the lad I brought in towards the end of the second half, Jason Hardy, did exceptionally well and I have to consider: do I teach Formby a lesson? At higher levels you can most certainly do that, because you're carrying a big squad. You can leave him out for the next game or the next two games. But the way I feel about it, big squad or not, I'm going to do it anyway. Besides getting a suspension and a fine, it's going to cost him his place and I think that will make sure the players in future realise their responsibilities to the football club and to their team-mates and don't make rash decisions on the pitch.

[The decisions to travel to Torquay and back in a day may, Docherty believes, have cost Rochdale more than they bargained for.] This is the difference between the big clubs and small clubs. The big would come down the day before or fly down. But, even knowing how the finances work at our club, I would have gone for an overnight this time. Considering the way we started the season it would have been worth the extra £1,000 to £1,500 to get the fans back. If we had come down yesterday, prepared properly and got the result we wanted, the cost would have been more than compensated for by the gate against Northampton on Saturday. It's all supposition, of course, but at the end of the day, it's a gamble well worth taking in my mind's eye.

Now we've got the long journey back. I've done this many, many times. You get back at three or four in the morning. Some of these players who have been here tonight are going to play in a reserve game tomorrow night because we're such a thin squad. The lads who came on as subs will play. It's very difficult to do anything else. But then I'd like to think that if I asked the entire senior squad to play tomorrow in the reserves they would play. That's a lovely feeling for a manager.

Me? I've got my stick-on smile, haven't I? There are positive points to be drawn from tonight, from the character and courage of the players. That encourages me greatly. It's the same with the feed-back I get from the players during training. I encourage them to knock on my door any time, be it professionally or personally. They might have a marital problem, a monetary problem or one of their kids might be poorly, and I try to work round that situation as much as I can. I'll give them as much leeway as I can. What I'm concerned about at the end of the day is that they give me 100 per cent on the field of play.

Contact is important, and it's the same with the chairman. I'm in contact with him almost on a daily basis. I keep him in touch with everything that is going on at the club and if I need anything done and done quickly, he has told me to just do it. There aren't many managers at any level, I believe, who can say that. The nice thing for me is that I can stand or fall on those decisions I make. He's been absolutely brilliant with me. I might change my mind later on . . .

The sentence is lost in laughs and he relaxes to watch another video or doze a while. There will be no stops for meals or toilets. The players have pre-packed sandwiches and a loo at the back. The coach does, however, pull up to drop off the Knutsford group.

'It's another example of the difference between the rich and the poor,' Docherty says. 'Take Man United, for example. Most of their players live in the Cheshire belt, Prestbury, that kind of area, within striking distance of the club, because United, like most major clubs, pay their moving expenses, solicitors' fees and the whole shooting match to get the players where they need to be.

'My club can't afford to do that, so I have players in Bradford, Leeds, Sheffield, Liverpool, Warrington and Manchester. We work around that and the players are prepared to travel at their own expense. We'll meet at Knutsford or other stop-offs. It's not just Rochdale

Football Club, there are many other clubs in the same situation.'

The rest are driven on to the M62, then the A627(M) spur for Rochdale and finally back to Spotland. It is 3.40am.

CHAPTER FOUR

Flogging a Dead Horse

A match foreseen as the final stepping stone to the summit of the Third Division completes Rochdale's week of despair. They lose for the first time at home, 2–1 to Northampton, and claim they are the victims of a gross miscarriage of justice. The referee overrules a linesman flagging for offside and Northampton plunder their decisive second goal. If you can't believe it, as they say, have a look in tomorrow's paper. There's the confirmation: Rochdale are mid-table.

All of which serves to arm the sceptics, those who question the acumen of the manager and the men who appoint him. Some register their dissatisfaction by simply staying away, others by verbal and written protest. The fanzine, *Exceedingly Good Pies*, repeatedly condemns the manager's tactics and gives a former director, Trevor Butterworth, the platform to present the board as unambitious and incompetent.

The fanzine also reveals that Rob Wilkinson, the would-be club PR man, has abandoned 'The Dale Dream' and taken a full-time job with Leigh Rugby League Club. He is reported as saying: 'It's very disappointing to leave

Rochdale without achieving what I came here to do, particularly after the Supporters' Club meeting, but after a few tête-à-têtes with Mr Walmsley, the feeling was one of slightly less regret. He didn't want me at the club at all.

'The feedback I got was that if the club took steps to try and attract people to games, they would come. Everybody at the club seems very apathetic towards the town as a whole. The club might have tried things in the past and it's not worked, but now they've given up and assumed that everybody in the town is not interested, and I disagree with that. They also take their existing fans for granted.'

Mass moaning is a football condition, of course, and is endemic at every level of the game. It is also a prerogative. At Rochdale they would settle for a few more moaners inside the ground. The attendance against Northampton was 2,193.

David Kilpatrick has seen and heard it all before, yet here he is, on a Monday lunchtime, back at the ground with Graham Morris and their Hornets counterparts for a Stadium Company meeting. 'Actually,' he says later, wandering through a suite overlooking the pitch, 'they're not the mavericks they used to be seen as.' He returns with an ashtray in his hand, sits and goes on: 'Relations are much better than they were.'

Kilpatrick, as we have already seen, is an experienced politician. Born in Leigh, in 1943, he has steered Rochdale AFC through some of its most torrid times and apparently survived with his sanity intact.

His first involvement with the club was in 1980, following one of the club's more infamous periods. Andrew Hindle had been chairman but the credit for keeping Rochdale in the League belongs no one quite knows where. The team finished bottom, eight points adrift of second bottom Crewe. In their campaign for re-election they faced stern opposition from Altrincham but edged the vote, 26 to 25.

However, two votes were not cast, the representatives concerned failing to arrive at the meeting on time. 'There was the famous quote where it was reported that Grimsby got lost in the traffic or something,' Kilpatrick relates. 'It's a bit difficult to believe, but there you are.'

Equally incredible was the scheme to solve the club's financial crisis. The ground was sold to an 'anonymous' buyer for £175,000 and loaned to Rochdale. It transpired the buyer was Euroway Cars, which was owned by the now former chairman, Hindle. Euroways was placed in the hands of the Official Receiver and the club revealed losses of £91,956 for the year.

Team affairs were no less eventful. Bob Stokoe resigned as manager the day after Morris joined the board and a matter of weeks before Kilpatrick joined. The following season Nigel O'Loughlin drove the team coach to Torquay and ended up playing. It was against this almost surreal backdrop that Kilpatrick became chairman, in 1982. He stood down to accommodate Tommy Cannon in the 1986–87 season, only to be reinstated in the summer of 1989 with the club still counting the cost of their brush with stardom.

Cannon's involvement seemed a good idea at the time. Kilpatrick says: 'I said "Okay, Tom, if you're going to be shelling out a few quid, it's only right that you become chairman." I just jacked it in. I resigned as chairman and then resigned from the board.'

After Cannon resigned Morris declared that the club was insolvent, with debts of about £250,000.

Kilpatrick's business interests were long concerned with the family granite firm and funeral directors.

KILPATRICK

Six years ago I sold the funeral business to the Co-op and five years ago I sold the granite business to a company in Aberdeen. I had a five-year contract to continue working with the granite business, in sales and marketing, and I've actually jacked in today. I'm going into a similar job with another company. I like to be in a team where you feel your corner is respected and that you really are part of the team. Over the past 18 months, two years, I've felt there was no future in it.

Here I feel part of a team, absolutely. I've been through some fairly busy times and carried on with Rochdale. There have been some dark moments and in your darkest moments you start to reflect. Again, on Saturday evening, you're left wondering how long you can keep going on not being lucky. Napoleon always used to say when he was appointing his generals, 'I know how good you are, but are you lucky?' You start to think to yourself maybe it needs somebody who's lucky.

When you start to look at it, though, we have made tremendous progress in the last six years or so. I have to discount the first five years I was involved because that was just survival. We were £400,000 or so in debt in '81/'82. Last year we made money, in the trading position. We had the Alan Reeves sale and I see nothing wrong in including the sale of players in keeping the balance sheet looking okay.

I think at the moment if we were really pushed we could move Paul Butler on. He's the best player we've got in terms of a saleable commodity. It would be absolutely heartbreaking to have to do it on the basis of a forced sale, but I think you could ring up several clubs now and say 'Look, we are in desperate financial difficulty, please make us a realistic offer for the boy'.

Kilpatrick made a much-publicised offer to resign if Rochdale failed to make the play-offs last season and was hounded from some quarters to keep his word. Fellow directors felt they had no one better equipped to take the chair and announced they had persuaded him to stay.

KILPATRICK
At the beginning of the season, there was a degree of frustration because we had been bombarded during the summer with bloody crap in the *Rochdale Observer* and I was going through a period when I was getting totally frustrated with the whole situation. I'm not too worried about the fanzine. I feel Francis Collins, who is the prime mover of the fanzine, is an intelligent young man but at times a little misguided.

Trevor Butterworth [a former director] has absolutely no credibility here at all. He was considered a buffoon by the players and he antagonised the staff. Having said that, I quite like Trevor. If he walked in now I'd have no problem talking to him. But Trevor just has this problem, this classic talent for failing to communicate, and he just becomes irritating.

When I told the supporters the club was skint the statement was made on two bases: firstly, to explain to the fans we would not be making major purchases during the close season; secondly, to alert Rochdale Hornets and the Council that we could not go on being bloody bankers for the Stadium Company, as we have been for the last two years. Every time there's been a major account needed paying it's been paid by the football club. We had to put £25,000 in to see us through July. We're living very much hand to mouth but we impose a discipline on ourselves that we will not trade with an overdraft.

The statement I made about resigning was fair, I thought, because sometimes the frustration of the spectators is that while the directors sack managers at will, they never look at themselves, and I'm not prepared to have that criticism levelled against me. I would have been quite happy to step down but I had an immense amount of pressure put on me from the Supporters' Club, from the Executive Club, from so many people, who said 'For Christ's sake don't jack it in'. Some of the letters were superb, saying they didn't want another Tommy Cannon or Andrew Hindle because the one thing we had got was a bit of stability. I thought these were genuine, heartfelt opinions.

The trouble is that people start to get an idea we can make £100,000 bids for players when the situation's never really changed. We still have gates of 2,000. You cannot get the message across to these people that we do not generate enough money through the turnstiles. The spectators we've got are absolutely bloody brilliant, but we just don't have enough of them. With those figures we don't break even.

We need money from the lottery, from our commercial operation, and then we need a big dollop from the central funds and ladder system now, from the League. And along with all that we need the bonus of a Coca-Cola second round. When you get into a deep depression by not getting through the first round of the Coca-Cola . . . It isn't only a game, it's a vital part of the bloody overall position of the club and we had a major setback, there's no question about that.

Yes, I have put money in personally over the years but I can't say how much because I don't think that's relevant and it's not very much. I think people are aware it's not something I really want to make too much noise about. If you're a Jack Walker, putting megabucks in okay, fine. Money's gone in at difficult times, from me and other members of the board.

I am not a wealthy man but then what do you mean by wealthy? If you work on a scale of Jack Walker and Alan Sugar, they're on another bloody planet. Okay, with one set of criteria I would be classed as a millionaire, but these days millionaires are two a penny and a lot of it is in investments, in property and so on. I can't turn property into 200 grand overnight. If I had £5 million at my disposal I don't think I'd be too upset about throwing the interest into Rochdale Football Club. But I haven't. I still have a young family, three kids. I've not got great dollops of cash I don't know what to do with.

For directors at this end of the League, it seems not only a matter of what you cannot put into the club but also a matter of what you cannot get out of it. Or is there something we cannot see?

*   *   *

KILPATRICK

I've got to say that the misery part is minimal, really, because if you start to work on that basis then you've got to get out of it. You have bad days. Torquay was a bad day. It didn't help having a player sent off. I can live with Rochdale getting beaten, for Christ's sake. My frustration comes from the fact that we are not in a position to do the things we want to do. That was a horrendous day – got to bed at five to four and thought to myself 'What a complete and utter waste of time that was – stuck in traffic, didn't do anything properly, the game was crap, we lost and came back home'.

The thing that really niggles me is that at Torquay we could easily have managed a draw. Then on Saturday we were absolutely garbage in the first half and I'm not so sure we would have sparked to life if this bloody nonsense with the linesman hadn't fired us up. But the fact of the matter is that over these two games we could quite easily have had two points. We got none.

And you're looking forward all the while. Lincoln have sacked their manager today and we play them on Saturday. Now the effect of that could go either way. You think Lincoln away Saturday, away to Fulham on the Tuesday, and then back home for Mansfield. Three games and you don't know how they will go. We've got an injury to Valentine, Thackeray and Shaw and it's 'Oh, my God, the squad's not right, it's unsettled . . .' That's the frustration.

Why do it? Good question. I think it becomes part and parcel of your life. You enjoy the good moments and you live with the bad. It's the involvement with the Football League. It's a hobby. It's certainly more of a hobby than bloody stamp collecting. But above all it becomes another facet of your life.

I remember when I joined the board I was told there was no chance whatsoever that Rochdale Football Club would survive. But we got back the ownership of the ground, cleared up all the debts, and we did it all again when Tommy Cannon left. The club had been losing £2,000 a week. Then when nobody comes along to take over from you, you feel a sort of responsibility. You've got to keep running the business.

I don't think we are a music hall joke now. I think we will always be painted with the big brush strokes, like 'we don't want to finish up like Hartlepool and Rochdale and Halifax' and all that sort of thing. But I think people who have been here now report good things about the club. Obviously we've not been very successful, we've got the longest run in the bottom division, I think, 20-odd years or whatever it is. That's a stick people can always beat you with and we've just got to live with that. But at least we're in the League – ask Maidstone, Newport, Halifax and one or two others about it.

I think people take a totally different view of Rochdale Football Club than, for example, Hereford United. Hereford came into the League and had that tremendous spurt up to Division Two and then back again. They've been rumbling around in the lower divisions for a long time since. But it's just the fact that we are Rochdale and the very name sounds boring. Hereford sounds so totally different.

I have a good friendship with Peter Hill, the chairman of Hereford, and that is another reason why you stay in the game, because you have met a lot of people and in the boardroom, with a few exceptions, you are all buddies. Mind, I was saying to Hilly on the phone this week that I'm now getting to the stage where if I find some of the visiting directors a bit boring I just can't be bothered. In the old days you made the effort, now I don't bother.

I don't think sacking the manager is difficult. I think if you've been as fair as you can be, a manager can ask no more. I think managers know when it's coming. Over the years I've parted company with a few managers. For instance, Peter Madden – I think that was the right time. I don't think he was thrilled at the time but he would admit afterwards that it was the best thing and we have become good friends again. Jimmy Greenhoff knew it was coming, Vic Halom knew it was coming. The only manager we've actually sacked since Halom was David Sutton and unfortunately – this is not a cop-out – I had to be in Germany the week we parted company with him.

Mick Docherty hasn't got a contract because I am totally and utterly opposed to managers having contracts. When Terry Dolan went to Hull we had to sue to get our £40,000. Contracts aren't worth the paper they're written on. You can argue it shows a lack of confidence, a lack of this, that and the other, but Michael has got certain employment rights anyway through the law of the land which would enable him to get a compensation payment.

Mick is proving himself. When he took the job on, I told him there was no contract but as long as he does the job properly he's okay, and I think he's doing a good job at the moment, and that some of the way he's playing is fine. He's trying to do things and I also think he's a good ambassador for the club, in the way he conducts himself and the image he portrays for the football club. His behaviour at away games is absolutely spot-on and I think that's important. So as long as he continues to do that he doesn't need a contract because as long as I'm here he'll not get sacked.

We gave Sutton a contract against my better judgement and that was pressure from the other members of the board because David was doing well and they said someone might poach him. I said fine, if they do good luck to him, we'll find another. At the end of the day – and this is where total cynicism creeps in – we finished up paying David Sutton £20,000 when he walked out the door as an abject failure here. Where's the benefit in a contract there? None at all.

So how will success or failure for Rochdale and Docherty be gauged this season?

KILPATRICK
Getting into the play-offs would be success. Super success would be actually getting out of the Division. Failure? If we finished bottom that would be total failure, wouldn't it? I don't think we'll talk about that.

Long term, you're not just talking about the prospects for Rochdale, you're talking about Bury, about Hereford, about Torquay, and even about Oldham, to a lesser extent because there are so many factors over which you have no control. You have to ask what our national game demands. Now, if it's a sort of German Bundesliga and bugger all else in terms of a structure of football below that, because that's professional and it produces good national sides, well, that's the best way to do it.

At the moment I believe there is a place for Rochdale as an integral part of the system, although how long that can continue I don't know, I honestly don't. We can only continue to operate at the level we try to operate at provided we are funded from elsewhere. If that funding were to cease then irrespective of what we thought, we at Rochdale would have to change, no question about it, we would have to go part-time.

I would like the League system to stay as it is. It would also be nice, in a way, to be sitting here in the old shed still, where the roof was leaking, the dressing rooms were falling apart, cinders around the place. I'm not saying we should stand still and I desperately want that end of the ground to be done. I think perhaps where this country has lost its way since the war is in the fact that our local stadia have not been considered the responsibility of the local authorities. You look to France and Germany and Italy and you realise what spectacular successes there have been there.

I suppose this is the only bit of an ego trip you can get out of it but I'd like to feel at the end of the day that what we can create here eventually adds to the civic stature of Rochdale – that instead of what we had here, which was the absolute pits, just rank, we are endeavouring to provide something about which people of the town can say 'It's nice at Spotland now'. 'Cos there's bugger all else in Rochdale, is there? I admit we've got a superb town hall, beautiful Georgian Post Office, very fine cenotaph, The Baum and Toad Lane, but after that, nothing. It is quite, quite awful, Rochdale.

I'm just saying, do you want the thing to stay as it is? I don't think we do. I think we're trying to take it on. We are trying to take the facilities into the 20th century and hopefully into the 21st century. We've got football, we've got rugby league and hopefully it can be a multi-purpose facility. There's no reason why you can't create the right facilities for people at a certain level.

It really is quite interesting that here we are, in the lower reaches of the Endsleigh League, and yet we are still able to attract people who want to sit in a box and want to sponsor games and want to be involved in it. How far do you want to be obsessed with always being the biggest and the best? There is a place in anything for doing what you do at your level to the best of your ability, and I don't see anything wrong in that.

I think because of the way life has become over the last 20 or 30 years, everybody is dismissive of everything. We've had to introduce new words to the English language to try and describe some things. Once you were a star, then superstar, now megastar. It's all media-led, all media hype that everything's got to be bigger, faster, longer. For me, that can be counter-productive in life. It is creating a lot of endemic problems that we have in this country because all it does is make people feel inadequate, it makes them dissatisfied with what they've got.

The very, very worst people on this earth are doing that – the people who produce television commercials. If ever you were made to feel inadequate when you can put a Rover 215 on the road for only £9,900, well . . . I mean, everybody's got £9,900 and if you haven't got that then you're living in some bloody igloo somewhere. Now that's been churned out every night to the guy who's getting 46 weeks social security money. Where does he get his 10 grand? From next door's garden?

It just fuels the reason why we've got a total breakdown in law and order. People find themselves in a situation where they don't have the chance to do it and at that stage you have to go route one – and route one is thieving, or at best blagging and borrowing.

I know that's a long, long way from the football ground but I think it's that set of values that you still have to bring in and say 'Well, this is what we're doing. We have nice people here, we don't have yobbos here, you can come here with your kids, you have no problems whatsoever. Even the spectators behind Sandy Lane don't cause trouble. Okay, the odd one may have had a pint too many, but it's not a problem and you can actually bring your family to Spotland.' Now isn't that worth something?

CHAPTER FIVE

Call Me Scrooge

The Lincoln conundrum is unravelled Rochdale's way. They win 2–1 and follow up with another valuable point from a 1–1 draw at Fulham. John Deary, the goalscorer and Dale's man of the match at Craven Cottage, came prepared. He has his celebration kit with him.

Docherty explains: 'I found 18 cans of beer in his bag on the way down and told him I was confiscating them. He pleaded with me, all innocent like, 'Why, boss, why? I've got one each for the lads.' As if. But that's Deary. I've known him for ten years and we know where we stand with each other. He's a character. He works hard and he plays hard. I'm not travelling back with the players because I'm staying down in London a couple of days, but I've no doubt he'll find a way of getting rid of those beers.'

A 1–1 draw at home to Mansfield is not so well received but Docherty is buoyed by a business transaction he sets up. He is negotiating to off-load his 'bad apple', Paul Williams, in an exchange deal that will bring Dave Lancaster back to Spotland from Bury.

Docherty says: 'I've got to speak to Willo but hopefully

we can pull this off. Okay, Lancaster is 33, 34, but he's got a good track record and we'll save money on the deal. All round, it's a good move for us.'

The defiant Williams does not consider it a good move for him and flatly refuses to join Bury. 'What could I do?' the manager asks. 'He didn't want to leave here and you can't blame him 'cos it's good at the moment.'

It gets better still. Dale have a rasping 3–0 victory at Doncaster and although they lose 4–3 at Lincoln in the Auto Windscreens Shield, the scoreline bears testimony to their capacity for creating and taking goals, which is confirmed when they win 4–2 at home to fellow promotion aspirants Exeter City. Even Williams plays a part, appearing as a substitute and supplying the pass from which Peake converts the fourth. Next on the agenda, an even bigger game: Dale, now fourth, travel to Gillingham, the Third Division's pace setters.

Rochdale's players and officials gather at noon the day before the match, for one of those rare treats, an overnight. The huge frame of Williams seems to fill the reception area but he will not be occupying a place on the coach.

'I've got a knee injury,' the man with a Northern Ireland international cap says. 'It's possibly a cartilage. I'm going for a scan. It's frustrating, just as I was getting back into it and the team is doing so well. It's been great. No one wants to be out but hopefully I'll be back soon. It's been great, the gaffer's been great.'

The irony is not lost on Docherty, whose attitude towards Williams has mellowed. 'In fairness to the big man, he's been knuckling down and anyone who delivers will get a chance at this club. It's the same for everybody.'

A blow for democracy is not how Docherty interprets the interim European Court of Justice verdict in the Bosman case, which directs that players should have freedom of movement, uninhibited by transfer fees, when their contracts have expired. 'It's all very well for people to say all we have to do is give our players long contracts, but clubs like Rochdale can't afford to do that. Only the Man Uniteds can do that. We could end up having to make wholesale changes every summer.'

Dave Bywater, one of those charged with ensuring the flow of young talent into Spotland, is on the floor of Docherty's office, grappling with kits. His familiar, beaming face lights up even brighter when Docherty shows him a letter from the father of an Under-15s team player. The boy dislocated a kneecap but, the father writes, thanks to the care and attention of Bywater, Hicks, Robson and Dawson, he is on the mend. 'It's nice to know the club is appreciated when it comes to looking after the youngsters,' Docherty says.

Docherty is conscious not all his endeavours are appreciated and the two goals conceded late in the match against Exeter rekindled the embers of resistance among the more pessimistic. 'I was disappointed from that aspect, too. It takes a bit of the gloss off. You try to be more professional, try for clean sheets, but people get a bit more casual when they know they've won the game. I was annoyed to go 4–1 down at Lincoln because they're not a good team and that was dire, but sometimes it serves as a kick up the backside.

'On the plus side we've scored 20 goals. There's only Swindon scored more in the whole four divisions, so that's encouraging. The thing I've tried to impress upon them more than anything is that we must get the ball into the box early. I'm not bothered what type of ball it is because it's got to be defended then. All in all, the club's going in the right direction. The youth policy is doing smashing and the first team is up there near the top.'

And for this match at least, they are conducting themselves like a top team.

'Having an overnight is absolutely brilliant. It enables the players to prepare as they would at home. They don't have to get up at seven or eight in the morning and travel four or five hours. We're staying at a four star hotel at Dartford Bridge. The lads will get a nice meal tonight. They've got leisure facilities, so they can have a swim if they want. Breakfast is optional, early morning is optional. Some like an early breakfast, some don't like breakfast at all. I used to love a lie-in. Hated having to get up.'

Docherty is inevitably beavering to the last although he can rest assured his stock is still rising with once-reluctant employers.

Michael Mace benignly acknowledges the blur of his manager, passing through to the secretary's office, and says: 'I think the best thing that's happened to this club in recent times is the appointment of Mick Docherty. I know it came about after a long and protracted period which did not show the club in a good light, but I think this was a sign from above. His attitude is marvellous. He doesn't grumble at the lack of facilities and money, he's just got on with it.

'He's made some very astute signings and he's got things organised, like a very good training team, and he runs the board brilliantly, which is the sign of a sensible manager. If any man deserves success it is

Mick Docherty. I just hope he does it, not so much for the fans or the team itself, but just for him. If it does come about, if we do get promotion, either directly or through the play-offs, then Mick Docherty will be the man to blame.'

A couple of miles from Spotland, another director, Graham Morris, is at his desk in the office of Wyatt, Morris, Golland & Co, Chartered Accountants. The financial affairs of Rochdale AFC are on computer here and, evidently, constantly on his mind. Without having the title, he is effectively vice-chairman and it was his opposition to the recruitment of a manager from outside the club that led to Docherty's appointment.

Morris says: 'Anyone coming in would have wanted to bring in his own people and that would have meant Mick and Jimmy going, which would have been immoral, and of course we would have had to pay compensation for dismissal. There was no way I was going to go along with a vote like that.'

He presents the scale of Rochdale's financial challenge in the meticulous detail you would expect of an accountant.

MORRIS
Take last Saturday's game. We're fourth now in the Division – attendance 2,052. The money on that is £7,266.50. Knock the VAT off, that gives us £6,184. After that we have to pay all the stewards, the girls in the office, the turnstile operators, and then you have to divide that by two because we get a home game only once a fortnight. That leaves you with less than £3,000 and with the wages bill now

about £10,000 a week – the players are on new incentive bonuses when they're in the top three or the top seven, something the chairman agreed to while I was away and I wasn't very pleased to discover when I got back – we're looking over our shoulders all the time.

We're not actually in debt. We are one of the few clubs in the Third Division who haven't got an overdraft because we keep things very tight. But things are getting out of hand because the gap between the small clubs and the big ones is getting greater and there's more and more pressure on the lower level clubs. We're now getting crumbs compared with the Premier League slice. We get about £4,000 a week from the pool, FA Cup, TV fees etc, and we've been making up to £3,000 a week from our lottery, but we're being hit by the National Lottery so we're taking a deep breath over that. Then there are sponsorship and donations, things like that.

We lost £37,500 in the year ending May 1994, and the only way you can make up the deficit is by selling players, so the following year we sold Reeves for £200,000. If all else fails, you end up dipping in your own pockets, though we've not had to do that very often. Despite our results, our gates are the third worst in the Division. Only Scarborough and Darlington are worse off and they are near the bottom.

When you go into a season you hope you might have a good run in the Coca-Cola Cup, and look what happens – we lose to York after extra time and they get Man United and make a fortune. We would have taken at least £150,000 from two legs with United. Our capacity is down to about 6,000 so we might have taken our leg to Oldham. All right, if it had been Leicester, it would still have been worth £50,000.

Even at this level of the game, catering for the executive and corporate clientele is a growth area. Executive Club membership is £350 for the season, private boxes £3,000. Rochdale have plans to continue improving facilities, but having the means to do so is another matter.

MORRIS
We are trying to develop the east end of the stand but it all takes money and we were badly let down by the Council over the building of the main stand. It wasn't supposed to cost the Stadium Company anything and we're left now with an overdraft of £450,000 on it, so we're having to pay the interest on that. It costs us £3,750 a month to pay into the Stadium Company to keep the stadium alive.

I asked for assurances from the Council that the building of the stand would not in any way put the soccer club in financial difficulty and I have letters from the Council giving those assurances. All the promises from the Council about the shortfalls being made up by sponsorship have produced nothing. Zilch. They offered us the benefit of their 'professional expertise' and then we get a bill for £15,000 from the Architects Department. When I challenge them they say their letter does not say they're not going to charge for it. That's sailing a little bit close to the wind. The hairs on the back of my neck stand up every time they send a rude letter threatening to stop this and that, or to sue. I think we've been let down exceedingly badly by our Council because other clubs we go to seem to get an awful lot of good deals.

I don't apologise for being frugal, but I have got to be a bit of an Ebenezer Scrooge in the club if I'm in charge of money. If anything's wrong, it's my fault, and if they get themselves in financial trouble that's my fault, as well. I can't win. I'm the nasty guy they all take the mickey out of. But I joined the board in 1980, when they were desolate, bankrupt, didn't own the ground, so I'm pretty well used to the way things are. Desperate times have meant desperate measures.

There was a fairly big scandal over the deal behind the sale of the ground back in 1980, and David Kilpatrick and I went to see this guy at Allied Irish Bank, in Manchester, with our knees knocking because we owed him £100,000 or so and we knew they could come down and impound our gate money. We put forward a proposal whereby he supposedly lent us the money, but of course no money would change hands and we would pay it back over a given period of time. Obviously we were clutching at straws because we didn't really have anything to offer him.

Anyway, we were called into his office, never met the man before. Big, long office, nice thick carpets, wood all round the side, and he had his solicitor –

the pinstripes and black coat type. We're thinking, 'Oh, my God'. But as we walked towards him he said [Morris affecting an Irish accent], 'Ah, to be sure, Mr Morris and Mr Kilpatrick, lovely to meet you. Come over here, we're having a drop of wine and getting quietly pissed. What would you like?' I thought I can't believe this. Not at 11 o'clock on a Monday morning. I mean, we owed him all that money. At the end of the day he said no, but at least he relaxed us.

We eventually did a deal in 1983 to buy back the ground for £60,000, which we borrowed from the Council. We also borrowed £20,000 from Greenall Whitley, cleared our debts and started again. I stood on the pitch with a bottle of champagne and my fellow directors actually drank a toast to me. I think that's the most appreciation I'll ever get!

Then Mr Cannon got involved and of course when you've not got a lot of money it's very attractive when someone comes along and says 'I would like to do for Rochdale what Elton John has done for Watford'. He was always telling us about the tax he was paying and wouldn't mind diverting things into the club because he loved Rochdale, but we didn't see a lot of money diverted. Any publicity, unfortunately, seemed to go to Mr Cannon, not the football club. We were mugs. So I quit first as I couldn't afford my corner and about three months later the others followed.

We let the man have his head but when Rochdale were bottom, losing 4–0 to Peterborough, and the crowd were chanting 'Cannon out, Cannon out', he left before the end of the match. He was absolutely furious and that was the last time he went to a game. Eventually we came back and got stuck into the mess again.

And then there was the sticky problem of the Pearl Street Snack Bar. The following letter speaks eloquently enough for itself:

23rd October 1986

The Directors,
Rochdale AFC,
Spotland,
ROCHDALE.

Dear Mr Morris,

ref: Pearl Street Snack Bar.

You have always been supportive and shown a welcome interest. I feel therefore, I should keep you in the picture regarding an unexpected and uninvited development which has left my wife Irene and myself feeling hurt and resentful.

We have been told by the Chairman of the Fighting Fund Committee that our services are no longer required unless:

(a) We mix sugar in our coffee urns and not have it in separate sugar dishes on the counter.

(b) We sell coffee only and discontinue offering tea.

Experience with visiting fans has proved conclusively that tastes vary in different parts of the country. An alternative to coffee is welcomed by many, hence we have sold both for quite some time.

Also, lots of customers prefer their beverages with little or no sugar.

Mr Jack Ashworth argues it slows serving if fans have to put in their own sugar. We have not found this.

It is not costing more – in fact the reverse, as fans will and do buy more if they get what they want. Jack Ashworth has gone on record as saying that fans at their bar 'get coffee with sugar in, like it or lump it.'

You probably feel, as Irene and I do, that this is so trivial as to be unbelievable. All we are trying to do is provide a friendly service and improve the image of Rochdale AFC, which we hope visiting fans will take away with them.

We are therefore convinced there is more to this than meets the eye, and that, although denied by Jack Ashworth, it owes more to the fact that from this season, Irene and I have sold Nicholsons pies instead of Hiltons.

This decision, agreed to albeit reluctantly by the Fighting Fund Committee, followed repeated complaints by myself and Mr Fred Kershaw, concerning the quality of Hiltons pies.

Nicholsons have supplied pies which are not brown and overbaked, and at a price considerably less than Hiltons, i.e.

Hilton	£2.88 per doz.
Nicholsons	£2.58 per doz. (meat).
"	£2.38 per doz. (meat & potato).

Purchases this season – Pearl Street Bar only:—

	Meat (dozs).	Meat & potato (dozs).
Crewe	5	5
Burnley	9	9
Northants	4	4
Exeter	2	2
Colchester	2	2
Watford	15	15
	37	37

These pies cost us:	£183.52.
If bought from Hilton:	£213.12.
Saving to RAFC, (one bar only, 6 matches):	£29.60.

What would this come to over a full season? (In addition, Mr Fred Kershaw has ordered and sold a small number of Nicholsons pies in the Main Stand Snack Bar.)

I think we should be astute enough to have more than one string to our bow – i.e. two bakers – this is normal commercial practice and keeps suppliers on their toes. This policy may unfortunately now go by the board with my departure.

I mention the pie situation because I strongly believe that such bizarre action by Jack Ashworth cannot possibly be put down to such a frivolous and petty reason as having sugar in sugar dishes!

In these times it is not easy to find workers willing to give their services free, and you may think it worthwhile to keep an eye on the future of the Pearl Street Bar.

I take the view that you are entitled to know what is going on. At least you now have the background to what is a most inexplicable affair.

We are not asking to be reinstated. My wife is too hurt to want to come back. As for myself, I know only one football club – the one I have supported for 49 years. I shall go on supporting the club in the only way left to me – through the turnstiles, and wish RAFC every success, especially in the new image which it is bravely attempting to project.

> Yours very sincerely,
> ALLAN ROBERTS
> SHAREHOLDER, MEMBER SUPPORTERS'
> CLUB AND FAN.

c.c. General Manager.
Public Relations & Commercial Manager.

The pressure seldom eases.

MORRIS
There's a lot of worry a lot of the time, both at the matches and away from them. There have been many sleepless nights, but there must be some fun or you wouldn't do it, would you? I enjoy the excitement of watching us go through to score a goal, just as any fan does, but then I sit there worrying in case the opposition come back and score.

We had a good win last week and yet a bad result

tomorrow will mean we still have only 2,000 next
week. When the crowd of 2,053 was announced
last Saturday the Exeter supporters jeered. They're
getting an average of 3,500 and they're in the
hands of the Official Receiver! The Rugby Club
are the same as us except they don't have to pay
wages during the summer. It's all about money,
this game.

Money is indeed the topic up for discussion on Monday.

MORRIS
We have board meetings only when necessary. We
can phone one another and discuss frivolities. But
when it comes to a situation where we've got to
pay this week's wages and no money is coming in
from the gate this week, we have to do something
about it. So there is a board meeting on Monday
and that will be the first thing on the agenda: how
we are going to pay the week's wages. Hands in the
pocket is probably the only way unless, of course,
we go to the bank, but the only way I've been able
to control the resources of this club over the years
is by not borrowing.

Morris drives to Gillingham on matchday accompanied
by his wife and, true to the Scrooge persona, immediately calculates the cost of a 1–0 defeat – and the
cost of simply being Rochdale, one of football's poor
relations.

MORRIS
A crowd of 7,785 brings in receipts of £40,000

because their prices are considerably higher than ours. Then you hear Man United have had 21,500 for a reserve game to see Cantona. That would bring in enough to keep us going till the New Year. What chance have we got? It's like banging your head against a brick wall. Thank God we're not in the bottom four. We'd go out of business.

The board again heeds Morris's advice about the perils of taking a loan but also wish to avoid the pain of inflicting on themselves another whip-round. So, Morris is deputed to ask the bank manager to 'hold off', pending the income from Saturday's gate, and not bounce the cheque to cover the wages. 'Unless we get about 4,000 at the match, though,' Morris says, 'it won't be enough.'

Nor is his plea to the bank. The director who missed the previous collection pays up this time and Morris calls Wimbledon for the latest dividends due on the Reeves deal. On top of the original fee, Dale receive £1,000 a game up to a total fee of £300,000. 'Trouble is he's missed a few matches through injury and that's bad news for us,' Morris says.

Docherty appeals through the columns of the *Rochdale Observer* for the locals to turn out in force and support Dale at home to Colchester. The response is a crowd of 2,193. 'What can you do?' Docherty says. 'I don't think they'll be convinced unless we are still in with a shout three games from the end of the season.'

Worse still, the match ends 1–1. And no one can blame Williams. He is recovering from a cartilage operation.

CHAPTER SIX

Upstairs, Downstairs

The last suggestion for a therapeutic day out would be a trip to London. Rochdale have made the trek to the capital 40 times over the past 88 years and never won. They have managed to stave off defeat in only seven of those matches. Now they head for Barnet. All right, so this is a club on the northern edge of the metropolis, a relative newcomer to the League, struggling to maintain that status. But it is still a trip to London, which ranks as marginally more appealing than a one-way journey to the Vauxhall Conference.

Early events scarcely indicate the course of history will be changed. Barnet hurl men and ball forward, Dale retreat. This time, however, the Londoners fail to break down the Northern resistance and, come the second half, a unique happening unfolds. Rochdale take over, run riot and gain their first capital success by 4–0.

Ray Clemence, the former England goalkeeper turned beleaguered Barnet manager, conveys his despair by saying he would not wish to show his worst enemy a video of the match. Mick Docherty would happily ogle every frame. 'Our performance, in the second half especially, was our best away from home since I've been here,' he declares.

Docherty's team go on the rampage again in the home Auto Windscreens Shield tie against Darlington with Paul Moulden's second-half hat trick in the 5–2 victory perfectly timed to secure him a permanent job at Spotland. The manager is spared the chore of lobbying the directors because they become aware Wigan are interested in the player and dare not allow him to slip away down the road.

'Mick hasn't held a gun to our heads,' Graham Morris says. 'We have to let him have Moulden or the fans would be after our heads.'

Moulden, who in the 1981–82 season scored 289 goals in 40 matches for Bolton Lads Club, duly signs for his seventh League club and Doc expresses his appreciation of the board who, he says, have been 'brilliant'.

Docherty's office might depict a fabled bootroom scene from football's past this Friday lunchtime. The lair is unpretentious with whitewashed walls, and desks and chairs presumably garnered from a second-hand shop. But it is rich in football banter, with members of staff and directors drawn in by the mood of optimism and excited anticipation.

Two important League games come up in the next four days, and beyond lies the FA Cup first round tie against Second Division Rotherham United, all at Spotland.

'You'd ideally like an easier draw and look to go on to the third round with the big boys,' Docherty concedes, 'but the players will be up for this and it's better, I believe, than being drawn away to the likes of Northwich or Altrincham.'

From the far side of the office, Michael Mace offers the

benefit of some archive information: 'We've got a good record in the FA Cup against Second Division sides. I seem to recall we beat Northampton when they were up there.'

Docherty leaves with Steve Walmsley in search of more comforting words and attention. 'Got to go off to the hospital,' he explains. 'I've been half eaten by bugs or something in training. See you later.'

More mirth. And, when the manager has vanished, more appreciation of his efforts. Jimmy Robson, organising the junior teams with the assistance of Dave Bywater, puts down the phone to tell his colleagues: 'When I go to meetings with other people in the game they all say "Hey, you're doing well, aren't you?" The next thing they say is "Who are your best players?" I tell them Peakey and Butler.'

'When anyone asks me,' says Mace, 'I tell them "Our best players are out of your price range". Killy doesn't want to sell anyone, anyway. He wants promotion. I reckon 80 points will do it for us. We've got 22 from 13 games so I'm sure we can get 80 from 46.'

Another director, Chris Dunphy, steps in and cranes his neck around the corner of the L-shaped room only to see the manager's chair is unoccupied. He wanted to ask Docherty if he would be willing to switch the home fixture against Preston, on Boxing Day, to Deepdale and play the return match, in March, at Spotland, by which time Rochdale expect to be able to accommodate more customers.

'I know what you mean,' Robson says. 'You're thinking of the financial side, aren't you? I don't know, though. You'll have to speak to Mick about that.'

Dunphy is optimistic business will look up. 'They'll

start to come back, now,' he predicts. 'They know it's not a flash in the pan. The town is buzzing. Two big home games to come, and if we beat Cambridge . . .'

Heads nod in agreement. The unspoken message is that a win tomorrow will set up a tasty encounter and, theoretically, an equally tasty pay night when Chester arrive here on Tuesday.

Elsewhere in the club there is less enthusiasm for the proposed switch of the Preston matches, lest they antagonise their own fans by depriving them of home fare on Boxing Day and because police already committed to duty at Blackpool that day would probably object. But the meeting with Cambridge goes according to Dunphy's plan. Dale win 3–1, Moulden setting them on their way with a goal after only four minutes.

By Tuesday another manager has lost his job. Don O'Riordan of Torquay, the longest-serving boss in the Third Division, has parted company with the club following their 8–1 home thrashing by Scunthorpe. Torquay had won only once in 14 matches and that – wouldn't it be? – against Rochdale. 'I'll get their chairman some After Eights when they come up here,' Docherty mischievously promises.

An hour and a quarter before kick-off against Chester, the atmosphere in the manager's office is still buoyant. If results here and at two other grounds go Rochdale's way, they could climb from third to top. 'I love big matches,' Doc enthuses. 'Great, aren't they?'

Robson is at Stockport, spying on FA Cup opponents Rotherham, and Bywater has looked in to offer any help Docherty may require. Occupying Robson's chair is Len Hilton, Spotland's answer to the Ancient Mariner. A club vice-president and former director, he regales all-comers with anecdotes of his evidently colourful and active past. He recalls football days in the forces, when a Lancaster Bomber took his team to away matches. 'Bloody 'ell,' Doc says, 'we could have done with one of those for Torquay.'

Hilton gives Docherty another chance to test his reflexes when he tells of his solitary appearance for Rochdale. 'I had the one game and never got asked again.'

'Must have been some game, Len.'

Hilton turns to a plate of sandwiches for consolation, revealing the tiniest of pigtails in his grey hair. 'You can tell Jimmy's not here,' he suggests as he picks at the clingfilm. 'He'd have gone through half of these by now. Anybody want one?'

There are no takers but Doc has a more recent story to relate. 'I went to see my lad, Matthew, playing the other day and as soon as I saw the referee I recognised him as the linesman from one of our matches. Sure enough, he recognised me, too, and came over and said, "Oh, no, not you – get back into the dugout." We both had a laugh.'

That reminds him. 'My daughter's coming tonight with her fiancé. Said I'd see her before the match. Excuse me. Won't be long.'

He isn't. 'Can't see her.'

He has, however, found an old Burnley chum, Colin Waldron, who is introduced to the 'bootroom'. Reluctant to sit, Doc paces his office and is conscious of the giveaway signs. 'Nervous energy,' he confirms. 'Think I'll just go and check on the lads.'

The lads presumably being fine, Docherty returns with Chester's teamsheet, sits at his desk and studies the names. 'I think they could be going five at the back. That's a compliment to us if they are.'

He gets up for the last time to rejoin his lads and deliver final instructions, good luck wishes accompanying him from his office.

Hilton still doubts a substantial increase in the attendance tonight. 'It's difficult, you see. It's not in vogue to support Rochdale, it's not the style, never has been. Everybody wants to be associated with big clubs. You even see them round here now in Newcastle shirts. Bloody Newcastle!'

Steve Walmsley pops in to enjoy the crack, 'just for two minutes'. So does Keith Clegg, the former secretary. He surveys the room and settles his gaze on the plate of sandwiches. 'Jimmy not here tonight?'

There remains, even now, something of an *Upstairs, Downstairs* syndrome in football and at the top of the stand, directors of both clubs, and their guests, take their seats with almost ceremonious timing, just as the teams are lining up.

The view for some is momentarily obscured as a family group are ushered from the public area to the home directors' box. By the time vision is restored a penalty has been awarded to Chester.

'What's that for?'

'No idea, couldn't see.'

'Sorry about that.'

'It's all right, don't worry.'

'Who are they?'

'Their son plays for one of our junior teams and he's a bit good. Trouble is, Man City are sniffing round. Got to look after them.'

Ah.

Somebody seems to be looking after Dale. It must be the worst penalty of all time, wide by almost the width of the goal. Chester also have a goal disallowed. The reprieve is only temporary. Chester, who retain an orthodox back four after all, are patently not here to contain, and midway through the first half they fashion a simple tap-in for Cyrille Regis. Yes, the very one. Amazing the people you bump into in the lower divisions. The former England striker and his midfield colleague, Gary Shelton, both 37, demonstrate that good old 'uns can always beat average young 'uns. Regis's nous presents Dale's defenders with constant problems and Shelton's poise and distribution govern the flow of the match. A shot blazed over the roof behind Rochdale's goal is a mixed blessing. 'That's another 60 quid,' Morris laments.

He is slightly consoled by the turn-out on a sympathetically clement evening. Scanning the all-seater stand, virtually full thanks to a vociferous contingent from Chester at £8 a head, he estimates: 'Mmm, just about 3,000, I'd say. We're having to put the away fans here because we've had to close the end behind the other goal on the orders of the safety officer. We've got to build a new stand there – that's another £1 million.'

The terraced Dale end is almost as silent as their team scurry in vain to gain a foothold. Chester somehow squander a double opportunity to extend their lead and a lone voice from the seats implores: 'Get it down. Find your man. Gerrem told, Docherty.'

Perhaps the manager heard. Now he is on his feet, barking orders. The natives stir at last, summoning the enthusiasm to air some of their chants. The unwritten law of the directors' box, of course, demands restraint and decorum, but make no mistake, they are fans in the posh seats, too. It's just that they wear ties and their ladies drape blankets over their legs. They moan and groan as much as the rest. Some, like Morris, kick every ball and wince at every tackle. They stifle their more extreme emotions but still applaud vigorously and, as is more often the case this evening, throw up their arms in dismay.

The stream of comment could be from any part of the ground.

'Get it on the floor. What the bloody hell's that?'

'Terrible ball, bloody stupid ball. Oh, God!'

'You wouldn't think it's the same team. They can't even pass the ball.'

'They've got some actors in their side.'

'Stupid bugger.'

Half-time comes as a relief.

'Sort 'em out, Doc.'

Docherty and the players disappear beneath the box as the directors pass through the main concourse into the inner sanctum that is the boardroom. The half-time analysis here is conducted over soup and coffee.

'Give us a chance,' a home director says to a smug visitor.

'They've got the midfield and aren't giving us a look-in.'

'Never liked this ref, but then never trust anyone from Merseyside. I should know, *I'm* from Merseyside.'

'We had Shelton here on loan a couple of seasons ago. Never did a thing.'

'I thought he looked good when he was here.'

A sheet of paper placed on a table lists the names of scouts and representatives from other clubs at tonight's match. There are 15 of them, including delegates from Arsenal and Nottingham Forest. 'They won't have seen much in our lot so far,' someone says.

A supporter leans into the box to greet the returning directors with the demand: 'Tell 'em to get it wide, get it wide.'

Quite how the directors are supposed to transmit this piece of advice to the team is unclear and that logistic would appear to be lost on the earnest patron, but polite smiles seem to suffice for now.

'I've known a supporter grab a chairman at another club by the throat and virtually pull him out of the box,' Morris recalls with understandable apprehension. 'And I've known someone being hit in the box. Our chairman's had a lot of abuse over the years but I don't think he's been subjected to physical violence yet. Mind you, he is six foot three!'

Kilpatrick is safe for another night. He is away.

'Be a different game in the second half,' Morris predicts. 'That's better,' he purrs as a player in a blue shirt finds another player in a blue shirt, a basic essential which generally eluded Rochdale in the first half.

'He's pulling him away, ref. Come on, got to be a penalty,' another in the box implores.

Hopes are deflated again when Rochdale fail to clear a corner and Chester score their second. Stony silence in the home directors' box, glee among the visitors, to the right, and delirium beyond, in the away fans' enclosure.

Dale are reduced to desperate punts forward, aerial meat and drink for Chester's lofty defenders against Moulden and Whitehall. 'It's no good up there.'

Morris, sitting on the back row, beneath a glass-fronted executive box, is passed a note, cradles it in the palm of his hand and nods. The attendance is 3,018, receipts nearly £13,000. 'Not a bad guess. Best gate this season. Mind you, there are quite a few from Chester.'

'Stupid bugger.'

Moulden is replaced by the bigger Thompstone, and Dale threaten to make inroads. Deary bulldozes his way through and is close to scoring, Chester miss a sitter, and then Peake pulls one back. The match is alive and for the first time Chester are a mite anxious. Even Big Cyrille is flustered. 'What's up wi' thi', Regis?' a home fan mocks.

Alas, before the recovery can take hold, it is over. Shelton restores Chester's two-goal advantage with a clean strike from the edge of the area and everyone in the ground knows the visitors' three points are safe.

'What a load of cobblers.'

'He's got the beating of Formby every time.'

'There's nobody in the middle at all.'

'How the bloody hell did he miss that?'

'We've no chance against these big buggers.'

'They're quick, aren't they?'

'Bloody rubbish.'

Rochdale are put out of their misery at 3–1, a drone of disenchantment trailing behind their homeward-bound supporters. Shaking heads distinguish the home directors from the chirpy visitors bound for the boardroom. A television positioned high in a corner of the room captures the demise of another English team in Europe and someone says: 'Liverpool are losing, as well.'

Mace tersely responds, 'Can't say I'm too bothered about them.'

Morris is similarly single-minded: 'Just when we get a decent crowd we let them down again. We were atrocious.'

He puts on a gracious visage for the Chester directors, shakes hands, says 'Well done' and ushers them in the direction of the pie, peas and red cabbage.

Docherty – a very different Docherty from the one who fizzed in and out of his office downstairs before the match – dutifully comes upstairs to show his face. He chats with a group sitting around a table but seemingly leaves a foot in the door. 'We got what we deserved. We didn't perform. After three wins on the bounce they sometimes get complacent. It's very disappointing. But we're back in on Thursday and we will start again. Listen, must go and find my daughter.'

He looks crestfallen, almost betrayed. This was the kind of big match he said he loved. His kids were here. His friends were here. And his team blew it.

Chester's manager, Kevin Ratcliffe, a distinguished player with Everton and Wales, cuts a contrasting figure: cool, composed, self-satisfied. He grips a pint, relives the highlights of the match with his even more self-satisfied directors, and eats a hearty supper.

Morris, happy the guests have been fed ('There's nothing more embarrassing than finding you haven't got enough food to go round'), now samples the pie and joins the huddle around the television, studying the other results and the revised Third Division table. Rochdale have slipped to fifth, Chester are up to third.

The visiting party reach for their coats and more hand-shakes. They also take with them a piece of Mace's special-ised humour: 'Don't come back.' They tell themselves he's joking, although one or two appear uncertain. He is probably none too bothered either way.

Rochdale's hospitality is renowned in football circles but some of the homeliness has been lost since the old, cramped quarters gave way to modern, spacious accommodation. As the chairman is wont to observe: 'The trouble is some people want the place even posher – fancy curtains and all that sort of thing.'

Entertaining is a prestigious part of inner football culture. Pride and honour are at stake every time you host a match. There is effectively a hospitality league table. 'Hereford have to be as good as anybody,' Morris acknowledges.

Down in Hereford, they acclaim Rochdale as among the most appreciative of guests. They fondly recall that following a typical pre-match repast, Kilpatrick ventured on to the Edgar Street pitch, answering the challenge to demonstrate his prowess from the penalty spot, only for his feet to slip from beneath him and consign him to prostrate ignominy. The fable recalls he was eventually wheeled away from the ground in a Tesco trolley.

Morris resumes: 'I'd like to think we make visitors welcome. The Scunthorpe people once called in to see us after playing at Burnley. We tend to have a reputation for our hospitality rather than our football!'

Last Saturday doubtless enhanced that reputation. 'I was here till half past ten,' the lady behind the bar says, 'and I was supposed to be going to a party at half past seven.'

That match ended at 4.45. It also ended in victory for Rochdale. This match ended in defeat and there is little appetite for a party. Just over an hour after the final whistle Morris is checking the bar bill and the staff sign off.

The bar at the far end of the stand is about to close, too, a handful of players, wearing their light green jackets, among the last finding solace. Deary, now beginning a three-match suspension after one too many brushes with officialdom, has no complaint about tonight's referee. 'You can't blame him for this result. That's down to us. We didn't do it. End of story.'

Outside, a couple of taxis wait to sweep up the remnants of the night. End of party.

CHAPTER SEVEN

Fan to the Grave

It is difficult for those who care about their game and, more particularly, care about their team, to comprehend life without this obsession. In the lower periods they might ponder a release from the hurt and humiliation, and consider the merits of carefree indifference. But then their team wins again, all evil thoughts are banished and their faith is restored. Docherty has got it right, the team have got it right. No worries. Fickle? Not us.

No one was lower than Docherty after the defeat by Chester but he picked himself up and chose Dean Martin and Ian Thompstone for the match away to their former club, Scunthorpe. They would be up for it, the manager figured. They would want to make a point. Smart thinking. Rochdale win 3–1, Martin and Thompstone contributing hugely to the success. So does Steve Whitehall, with two of the goals.

Even 'Scrooge' Morris is caught up in the 'here we go' mood. Over lunch with the bank manager, he finally bites on the extravagant course of taking an overdraft. The bank can no longer accommodate stalling tactics and the club have to believe that now they are on their way, that the money will come in. A board meeting agrees to a £75,000 overdraft, granted on the strength of personal guarantees from the directors.

Morris says: 'We can't go on having whip-rounds and the alternative was to sell players to pay the rest. We've decided to take the risk and go for it. If it goes really wrong we know the consequences.'

The board comes under more pressure at a fans' forum. Someone in the throng wants to know what happened to the £200,000 raised from the Alan Reeves transfer. There is, running through the ranks of the supporters, a vein of suspicion that the directors have creamed off their share. Kilpatrick acknowledges this as a good question, and then with a nifty piece of footwork any of the players would have envied, sidesteps the tackle and plays a reverse pass to Morris. 'I think that's one for our financial director.'

Morris, off-balance, feels the full weight of the tackle. 'Well . . . our wage bill is now up to £11,500 a week,' he mumbles while endeavouring to climb to his feet.

The tenacious fan is not going to be repelled so easily. 'What about the £200,000?' he demands to be told.

Morris goes down on his haunches and asks for attention from the physio. While the game goes on, he does his sums, totting up the transfer fees and signing-on payments incurred since Reeves' move. He comes back on to the field waving a bill of £110,000.

Still the fan lunges in. That does not account for *all* the £200,000. Morris, however, has recovered some of his composure and familiarly fluent style, and adds that there are, of course, other bills, overheads and those ever-increasing wages that have drained the rest. He just about salvages an equaliser. Especially when, as his coup de grace, he adds 'Haven't you noticed, five of the directors have got Jaguars. Only poor old Mike Mace drives around in a clapped-out car.' The rest of the encounter is a relative cruise, Docherty and the board emerging generally unscathed, and almost all have smiles on their faces by the end.

Mace, in any case, has no problem responding to those who suggest the directors have been taking money from the Reeves deal out of the club. 'I always say I never take more than £10,000 a week out of the club,' he states with typically provocative and ambiguous intent.

The club have a more resounding victory to savour in the first round of the FA Cup. They are three up by half-time against Rotherham United of the Second Division, and lead 5–1 with nine minutes remaining. Rotherham claw back to 5–3 and condemn Dale to a desperate finale, but that is the way it stays and Spotland explodes in relief. Better still, the draw for the second round gives them another home tie, against Darlington, a side they have already beaten twice this season. No one is prepared to shout it, but the message is clear: third round, the Promised Land, beckons.

The day before the visit of Hereford United in a League fixture, Jimmy Robson is sitting at his desk, taking some ribbing from the Doc about his reserve team striving to keep up with the seniors. They won a midweek match 7–4, despite having gone 2–0 behind. 'We were one down in 10 seconds,' Robson says. 'And this after we said we wanted to keep it tight!'

For one player in particular, it was a productive recovery. Darren Ryan, scorer of five goals, has been recalled to first-team duty for the game against Hereford in place of the injured Mark Stuart. Stuart was caught in the face

97

by an opponent's knee during the Cup win and lost two teeth, which was painful enough. X-rays now reveal a fractured jaw, which will have to be wired up and will keep him out of action for perhaps 10 weeks. So Ryan, regarded as a bit of a 'problem player' who does not make full use of his talent, is in.

Docherty says: 'I've given Ryno a talking to. I've told him it's up to him how long he stays in the first team. He's got his chance and he should make sure he doesn't let himself down or his team-mates down. I've given it him straight.'

The manager, having got his house in order, excuses himself to sort out another. 'I'm moving in this afternoon, so I'd better get off. See you later, Jimmy.'

He does not see Jason Peake until 20 minutes before kick-off against Hereford. The midfield player telephoned to say he had been held up in traffic so Docherty, unaware what time he would arrive, plays safe and names him among his substitutes. Peake is brought on in the second half but cannot lift his side, who fail to score for the first time in eight matches and have to settle for a point.

The inquest is still being conducted the following Thursday evening, as club officials mingle with some of their better-heeled supporters at a sportsmen's dinner for the benefit of the Centre of Excellence.

'We should have had a penalty.'

'Tell me about it,' Docherty says. 'And what about Thommo's miss?'

'They had 10 defenders back. Not easy.'

'A season or two ago we would have lost a match like that.'

'You can't score five every time.'

'I told the players, at least we didn't lose,' Docherty returns. 'We kept a clean sheet and we've got another point.'

Docherty is less comforted by another late arrival. He reveals that Ryan, the player he gave a 'talking to', turned up for training past the appointed hour and will suffer the consequences.

'That's the seventh time he's turned up late for training. I fined him, and told him to go home and that he wouldn't be going with us to Plymouth. I went spare. I've given him some leeway, told him if he wants to live in Wrexham that's up to him. But I've got to think of the other players. It wouldn't be fair to them to allow him to keep getting away with it.'

Two late shows in a matter of days understandably disturbed Docherty. 'Peake's been fined as well, but what puzzles me is why players don't give themselves more time, just in case. We all know traffic can be bad, so allow for it.'

The circle of privileged listeners nod in agreement. Fans make a serious commitment and have no respect for shirkers. The real diehards among them engage in earnest conversation with Robson about the latest reserve game. You have commitment, and then you have *commitment*.

By now the boardroom lounge is heaving and everyone is grateful to be called into the main suite for dinner. Almost 150 ferret around for their places and then respectfully stand as grace is said by the MC. The MC? Mick Docherty. It seems that the regular MC at these occasions cannot abide tonight's comedian, Ivor Davies, so the Doc of all trades volunteered to fill in. 'You won't be paid, though,' he was warned.

The menu is as imaginative as some of the football in the Third Division – prawn cocktail, beef and chocolate gateau – but the atmosphere is convivial and the feelgood factor embraces the entire company. Docherty has a captive audience, ('He wouldn't have been able to do this last season,' someone says) and appreciative comment flows from the diners as freely as the Mouton-Cadet.

'Not just with hindsight, but I said all along that instead of pratting about they should give the job to Docherty, and he's delivering. We're playing good football and getting the results. His man management is superb. I was talking to Valentine, who as you know was off injured for a while, and he was telling me: usually when you're out injured the manager only wants to know when you're going to be fit; the Doc asks how you are and tells you to come and see him if there's ever anything you need.'

There are also compliments for Les Duckworth, the marketing and promotions manager. 'Nothing's too much trouble for him. You ring him up and say you'd like to buy some tickets in such and such an area and he'll bend over backwards to sort it out for you. Just try it, you'll see.'

And, wonder of wonders, there are even good words for the board. 'They've taken a lot of flak, but they've kept the club going and now we're turning the corner. Kilpatrick's had to put up with a hell of a lot, but his heart's in this club and always has been. There was one match when we got a much bigger crowd than usual and he was outside, assuring everybody in the queue that the kick-off would be delayed and they'd not miss anything. And it was pouring down. He got soaked. And look at him, he's loving it now.'

They're all loving it, these local boys made quite good, professional and business people who haven't grown too big for their boots or their club. 'I've been coming here since I was five. There was a turnstile in that corner and there was like a dip in the ground underneath it, and I used to crawl under.'

'Or we'd climb over t' fence at that end.'

They are paying back their dues now. They are executive club members and box holders and matchday sponsors. And for that they get closer to directors, officials and players. Some even have a nodding acquaintanceship with the manager. They wallow in the perceived status.

Frank Duffy, funeral director, former mayor of Whitworth, a neighbouring township, and chairman of the Supporters' Club, is as familiar a figure behind the scenes at Spotland as he is on the terraces. He is afforded the cordiality of a powerful shop steward, and for much the same reasons.

'Brought the lad to see the greatest goalkeeper of all time,' he says. 'Well, I think he is, anyway.'

There would be few here, if any, willing to dispute Duffy's assessment. And yet, when he gets to his feet – not a giant of a man, as most modern goalkeepers are – and grinds out his routine, he cuts a rather sad figure. The jokes are strained, the delivery weak. He makes fun of the fact he has only one eye, the other lost in a car crash which effectively ended his top-flight career. It doesn't come over as funny at all. But then Gordon Banks is not a naturally funny man and no one here expected him to be. They would have been happy with unfettered nostalgia, spiced with more credible anecdotes. If, as he says, he is condemned to the after-dinner circuit by financial necessity, surely he would be better off sticking to '66 and all that, and, of course, that save from Pele. Leave the jokes to the funny men.

Whatever the regular MC's reservations about Ivor Davies might be, it has to be said he is a funny man.

Crude, yes; a pocket-sized Bernard Manning. But when you book him you know what to expect and you get it. At least the regular MC would not have been the butt of his opening gag. Davies, glancing at Docherty, says: 'I've never had anything against your dad, apart from the fact he didn't run off with my missus.'

And on it goes . . .

Docherty, undaunted, is back on his feet to conclude proceedings, throwing out – literally – the raffle prizes and then conducting an auction which reaffirms the loyalty of the gathering. Three signed footballs come under the hammer: the Manchester United ball raises £100, Newcastle United's £80 and Rochdale's £140. Try to make sense of that beyond these walls.

Formalities over, the Doc completes his duties by exchanging pleasantries with punters en route to the door and has a final reminder for Kilpatrick about tomorrow's trip to Plymouth: 'Ten o'clock, chairman, or we go without you.' Docherty smiles and Kilpatrick smiles, but the manager says he means it and the chairman knows he has to mean it.

Another employee, Steve Walmsley, is more circumspect when he approaches Kilpatrick. Just as well, given recent events. Walmsley was carpeted after a written complaint from the telephone company about his manner and language during a conversation with one of their employees. Walmsley evidently got the message. 'I frightened the life out of him,' Kilpatrick says. 'He's good at his job – but there are limits.'

On this evening, Kilpatrick is more like a doting uncle than a Draconian boss. He relives the highlight of his recent trip to Cyprus: following the team's progress to victory against Scunthorpe courtesy of the BBC's World

Service while subjecting himself to suitable inebriation. 'Bloody great, it was.'

These are times to be savoured and the tasting goes on at the boardroom bar. A pay bar, mind. One of the football club's handicaps as compared with the rugby club is that they have to abide by stricter drinks regulations on matchdays and Hornets, despite attracting smaller crowds, make more from bar takings.

According to one member of the present company, Hornets' directors argue and fight more readily than their counterparts at the football club. Whether there could be any link with relative liquid intake is open to conjecture.

What does surface now is Kilpatrick's lingering disdain for Hornets. 'Petty, small-time and not even in our league,' is the general drift. Kilpatrick recounts that he once calculated, in response to a rugby club official's question, that the effective weekly pay to a certain player was £700. The startled rugby man then asked how they managed it. 'With great difficulty, I told him. But we have to. They don't have a clue.'

A National Lottery grant of £120,000 will help fund the training facility that is to be incorporated in the development of the closed end at Spotland, currently a redundant terraced enclosure and grassy bank. Kilpatrick and his colleagues are still working at the rest, but then they have moved mountains, not just grassy banks, to get this far. 'I was told 15 years ago, when I came here and the club had debts of £425,000, that I had no chance of saving Rochdale. We're still here, though, and we're not doing badly, either.'

Even so, what a difference an FA Cup windfall would make. 'If we were drawn at home to United, or Liverpool, or Newcastle, there's no question, we'd take it away. Have to. If it's a Wimbledon, a Southampton, maybe not. That would be different. The thing we're trying to avoid is selling players. We could probably sell Peakey now for £750,000, but we don't want to. What a left foot.'

Darlington, of course, might care to spoil those Cup fantasies. And before that tie, Rochdale have two tough matches away, against Plymouth in the League and at Second Division Chesterfield, in the Auto Windscreens Shield.

'We could have done without the Chesterfield game during next week,' Kilpatrick says. 'We tried to get it changed but we couldn't. I said to Mick we ought to try and do something a bit different before the Darlington match. It's a very important day for everyone at the club so let's treat it as a bit special.'

Two or three days away in the sun, perhaps?

'Well, I was thinking more of laying on lunch before the game.'

A customary feature of the preparation will be Robson's report on the opposition. He will watch Darlington at Chester and miss the trip to Plymouth. If the chairman does not want to miss it he might be advised to summon a cab. It is now almost 3 am. 'Good God, is it really? Yes, better be off. I've got to be back here at 10.'

The trip is unrewarding. Dale lose to two second-half goals, mustering just one attempt in reply. They remain fourth in the Third Division standings, immediately above Plymouth, but one point and no goals from two matches represents a mini slump and, compounding the anxiety, Peake returns home nursing a hamstring injury.

Much as Rochdale could have done without the match against Chesterfield, it does at least provide Docherty with an opportunity to reshape his team ahead of the FA Cup tie. Stuart and now Peake sidelined, the Doc must soldier on without his two most creative players, and despite suffering a bout of flu. He stays at home on the Monday but reports for the trip to Derbyshire. 'I've been dreadful. Shivering, throwing up, the whole lot. I should still be in bed but I've got to be all right, haven't I? There's a job to be done.'

Now if you are the manager and you do not have an army of assistants then it really should take an awful lot to keep you away. But if you are a fan, who makes that long haul down to Plymouth and feels pretty disgruntled about the performance, and doubtless does not have a Swiss bank account, and certainly will be at the Darlington game, do you really need to be turning out on a dank Tuesday evening in late November to see an Auto Windscreens Shield tie? At Chesterfield?

In remarkably many cases, the answer is apparently 'Yes'. Compulsion? Sympathy? Fever? Dementia? For whatever reason, an almost full coachload of them set out on the official Supporters' Club trip. Far more will make their own way over the Pennines.

News of Docherty's malady prompts discussion about a threatened epidemic. 'Good. Could be more business for me. I don't mind working at Christmas.' The unseasonal sentiments are those of Frank Duffy, chairman of the Supporters' Club and, of course, an undertaker. Presumably it helps to have a sense of humour in that line of work.

The most striking feature of the clientele on the bus is how normal they are. No raging drunks, no obnoxious yobs. Just normal people. Frank's two sons are on board, there's Nigel, in shirt and tie, who collects the fares, there are fathers and sons, fathers and daughters, middle-aged ladies, elderly gentlemen.

A teenage girl is absorbed in her personal stereo and *Les Miserables*. A small boy is reading a book and deciding which shirt to wear. Yes, the away strip. Green. Many are intently working their way through sandwiches and hot drinks. Since smoking is now banned on board, the local 'scoop', Les Barlow, has sought alternative means of transport. One of the elderly gentlemen appears to compromise by sucking on his unlit pipe.

Nigel is also the resident film-maker and this evening he presents, as the in-ride entertainment, his coverage of a match earlier this season. There is no commentary. In fact, there is no sound. 'Nigel forgot to turn the sound on,' a voice gleefully informs the rest. 'This, for those who don't know, is the Exeter game.'

The match, won 4–2 by Dale, conveniently ends soon after the coach is met by a police outrider, who will escort this presumably vulnerable or dangerous cargo of humanity to Saltergate. Those on board are used to the procedure and accept it without concern or insult. This is a legacy of the lunatic age and no one, quite reasonably, dare pronounce that age over. Anyway, the bizarre structure over there is the Crooked Spire. Time to think about the match. Get your coats on.

Outside the ground, the atmosphere could not be said to bristle with the electricity of a big match, but then this could not be said to be a big match. Less than half an hour from kick-off, stewards and programme sellers outnumber customers. Some of the younger males in the Dale contingent dutifully stand, arms outstretched, for the frisking routine at the turnstiles and again, no offence is taken, no hostility sensed.

On the open terrace that is the away end at Saltergate, all is equally low key. Supporters congregate around the open hatch of a wooden shed from which homely ladies dispense refreshments. Duffy, plastic cup of tea in hand, stations himself at the top corner of the terrace and is greeted by everyone who passes his concrete perch. One supporter arrives late, clutching a Cornish pasty. 'Got lost in bloody Sheffield,' he feels compelled to explain, and moves along to claim his perch. Not a problem tonight. Still plenty left.

Duffy says: 'These are the diehards. You'll see them at just about every match. Dale is their team, that's all there is to it. It's easy to support a big club but not so easy to stick to a team that have been in the bottom division for so long. There again, it can be very expensive to follow a Premier League team, especially if you've got a family that like to come to the games. Trouble with doing well is you get yobbos wanting to jump on the bandwagon. We won't have troublemakers on our coach. They're all decent people who come for the football.

'I try to get to all the games I can, and some reserve games. I have to see the wife sometimes, though! She's not interested in football. I used to go years ago and then started going again with the lads.'

Duffy was asked to exercise his political acumen when fans claimed that some of them were being victimised by over-zealous police officers at Spotland. He reported the incidents to their superior and was assured 'they will be on car park duty from now on'.

His advance to the chair of the Supporters' Club was perhaps inevitable and he vowed to rebuild bridges with the directors. That process is on-going and the fans set themselves a £10,000 target to help fund the signing of

Moulden. The first £3,000 went on an executive box and at every home game the eight seats are sold to members at £10 each. Dinners and other moneymaking schemes are on the agenda, but not just for the benefit of the football club. The fans also support the local hospice and other charities. 'It's important to be doing something in the community, not only for the club,' Duffy reasons.

Right now Duffy's attention is held by Rochdale's efforts on the Saltergate pitch. 'We generally do well against these. Mind you, without Peake and Stuart we haven't got anyone to hold it, spread it about in mid-field.'

Dale are soon doing well enough again. Their fans follow the arced flight of the ball from Whitehall's left foot to the underside of the bar and in. The sprinkling of diehards celebrate and incur the requisite abuse of those Chesterfield supporters positioned adjacent to the Dale end, which their team are attacking in the first half.

'You have to expect a bit of that,' Duffy cheerfully concedes. 'This is not too bad, though. It can be a lot worse.'

Half-time and Rochdale still lead 1–0. Chance for another cuppa. Nice thing about a game like this is that you do not have to queue half an hour to get served – or get to the toilet. Not so nice is that you are open to the elements and during the break spots of rain patter the uncovered steps.

'If the heavens open, we get wet. Simple as that,' says Duffy, zipping his wet top. 'You learn to come prepared.'

A similarly prepared middle-aged woman produces a fold-up umbrella from her bag of tricks, but mercifully, for the bulk of the exposed Rochdale faithful, the rain ceases. They get a clearer view of Chesterfield's recovery. A shot cannons down from the underside of Rochdale's bar and out. 'We'll never score toneet,' a steward solemnly informs Duffy.

'Hope we can count on your local knowledge,' is the reply.

They can't. Thirteen minutes from the end, Chesterfield equalise. The noise of a thunderclap, generated by the extra home fans who made their way to the far end at half-time, and an accommodating roof, travels the length of the pitch and batters the heads of the Rochdale supporters.

Suddenly the moaners are back in business. 'He shouldn't be on the field,' a disgruntled fan declares, pointing towards a hapless Formby.

Duffy throws his eyes to the heavens.

Chesterfield fans throw the old one at the opposition: 'You're not singing any more.' In truth, Dale's choral repertoire hasn't been much in evidence all night. Still, wind-up taken.

The subdued travelling fans are contemplating the novelty of sudden-death extra time, but not for long. Gray half comes to meet a cross from the right, then retreats, and Chesterfield score a second. 'That side *again*!' the dissident roars.

The malcontents now have their chance to release some bile.

'That's rubbish, total crap.'

'You lazy bat.'

A late, rash challenge by Butler brings a booking and more concern. 'That means a suspension,' Duffy says. 'Two matches, I reckon.'

Butler need not worry about missing matches in this

competition. The referee blows up and Rochdale are out. Most of their followers are resigned to the outcome and are seemingly none too distressed. It is as if they came here out of a sense of duty rather than any deep conviction or desire for victory. They turn up no matter what, because that is what real football fans do.

Some make for the gates immediately, some stand and observe the ritual of exchanging applause with the players. And then they are all gone, summarising on the hoof, into their cars and on to the supporters' club coach.

'They're not bad, to be fair. They are a Second Division side and you can see why.'

'We couldn't expect to hold them in the second half.'

'At least we played some football tonight. A lot better than Saturday.'

'We had a better shape with two up.'

'We've got sorted for Saturday. That's the big one. We need to win that.'

The police outrider leads the coach from the ground, away from the town centre, on to a dual carriageway, and peels off. The coach is almost silent. There is no evidence of mourning or grief, or any emotion at all. Just silence. The passengers watch a film, finish their sandwiches, listen to music, or fall asleep. At 11 o'clock they are back at Spotland. Another evening in their lives supporting Rochdale FC is over.

CHAPTER EIGHT

This is Dreamland

It could appear only in a local newspaper: 'The club advises fans to get their tickets as soon as possible to avoid disappointment.' Perhaps it could be only in Rochdale. This is the second round of the FA Cup, Dale have a home tie, against a side they ought to beat, then it's bring on United or Newcastle. There shouldn't be a spare seat or square foot of concrete in the ground. Dream on. Get back to the real world. This is Rochdale. Heard it all before. Besides, it's Darlington. See how you get on Sat'di, eh?

To Dale's relief, Peake appears to be getting on well and defying what is now described as a medial ligament strain. He will be back in the side. So, too, will Valentine, having recovered from a viral chest infection. Bet neither of those ailments existed when 'get your tickets as soon as possible to avoid disappointment' was a trendy slogan.

A crowd of 3,732 avoid disappointment, as do Dale, in the nick of time. Deary, combative to the end, equalises twice, the second coming in the 85th minute, and his below-par team-mates are fortunate to have another chance.

'We've got to admit we got out of jail,' Docherty says. 'We weren't at our best and overall they were the better side. We were a bit tight in the first half and I had to crack the whip. We improved in the second. The one thing I can always count on is our fighting spirit and we showed that again today, no one more so than Deary. Two good goals. We've got to go away now for the replay and we're still in the Cup. We've got to be thankful for that and make the most of our luck.'

You would expect the Darlington camp to be abuzz with excitement and anticipation. Surely, they are justified in believing, they now have the measure of Rochdale and will finish them off at home. A third-round place has to be theirs. The commotion in and around the visitors' dressing room, however, sounds less like celebration than recrimination.

Suddenly, David Hodgson, the manager, or 'joint director of coaching', as he is fancifully called by Darlington, emerges and declares he has quit his job, whatever they want to call it. 'There's too much in-fighting,' he says by way of an explanation, except that non-regular Darlington watchers haven't a clue what he is on about. Bizarre? Surreal? How about the magic and romance of the FA Cup?

As Hodgson disappears into the night, the Darlington intelligence service reveals he had handed in his resignation before the match in frustration over the club's 'sell and don't buy' policy. He threatened to walk out a fortnight ago but managers do that from time to time to let off steam. They know the score down at this level and take it back. This time, though, he seems to mean it.

The FA long since abandoned its Monday lunchtime

wireless slot for FA Cup draws and the tantalising imagery of clunking balls in velvet bags. Television destroyed the image and now they have destroyed the velvet bag. The draw for the 1995–96 third round is more like extra time in the National Lottery. It is to be held on the Monday, but at around 10.30 at night and the crinkly old administrators pairing the teams have been replaced by crinkly old personalities, Denis Law and Terry Venables.

Law is suitably irreverent with his 'Oohs' and 'Aahs' and an invited audience (can't see anyone from Dale in there) giggle along. But where's number 48, Darlington or Rochdale? This is no laughing matter, this is deadly serious. A fortune, a dream is at stake here. On and on it goes and even Denis gives up on some of the more boring ties. You just *know* Rochdale are going to get one of those. Out come Liverpool. Lucky Liverpool. Another home draw. 'Will play Rochdale or Darlington.' YYY-E-SSS!

Can you believe they carry on? The world should be standing still to acclaim this. Do they not understand down in the Smoke what this means up here? What's the matter with them?

The directors, in the middle of a board meeting, at the Broadfield Hotel, leap in undignified celebration. A picture of middle-aged men behaving badly.

In the scattered homes of players and other officials and in the homes and pubs of the diehard supporters, yelps of ecstasy accompany ramrod arms and clenched fists. And, as if to prove the magical powers of the FA Cup, the urge of emotional involvement instantaneously overcomes hundreds more homes in and around the town of Rochdale. Life-long supporters. Course they are.

Docherty's senses are tugging him every which way.

'You hope and pray you get something like this but another feeling tells you it's not going to happen, not to you. It still might not. Darlington will be thinking it's for them. But if we needed any incentive for the replay we've got it now. It's up to us.

'It's great for the players and I don't have to tell them what an opportunity this is. They are Third Division players and they know they may never get the chance again to play against a team like that in a stadium like that. It's a million miles from our world. And for me it would be the chance to pit myself against Roy Evans. It's an unbelievable experience for all of us. The excitement is difficult to explain to anyone who doesn't know what it's like in the Third Division.'

Docherty, conscious that his own excitement is in danger of getting the better of him, pulls up sharply and turns on the professional jargon: 'But we can't afford to think about that because first we've got a replay at Darlington and they will be just as determined as us to get to Anfield. And before that we have important League business to attend to.'

That business resumes at Spotland the following Saturday, against Doncaster Rovers. 'I'm sure the players will be concentrating on winning the three points. If there are any shirkers they'll be out of the Cup tie.'

Those life-long followers are not quite ready to venture from their armchairs to see the game against Doncaster Rovers, and the 2,168 who take the trouble return to theirs with mixed feelings. Not a pretty game and Dale, who include on-loan winger Neil Mitchell for the injured Thompson, take a buffeting. But Whitehall converts his sixth penalty of the season – his 16th goal in all – and Rochdale have the points they wanted. Business is business.

Big business is now in the offing and all thoughts can switch to the FA Cup. Butler is suspended for the replay at Darlington but Docherty pointedly makes light of his absence. 'We can cope and I have no hesitation in playing young Bayliss.'

Cope they do. Bayliss defends heroically, as does the first-half substitute, Alex Russell, and anything that eludes them is repelled by the excellent Gray. The goalkeeper's composure soothes the nerves of the management and inspires his colleagues to conjure a winner. Barely 10 minutes from the end of normal time, Thompson, back in the team with the aid of a pain-killing injection, beats his man, checks, beats his man again and crosses for Martin to score. Darlington have no response and Dale can glimpse the famous sign that confronts the teams as they enter the Liverpool tunnel: 'This is Anfield'.

The vision is briefly obscured at the end of the match by the invasion of a rabid mob apparently seeking out visiting supporters to exact vengeance. Police and stewards intervene but the players are diving for the safety of the dressing room and their celebration with the fans is denied them.

Still, if you are looking for consolation, how about Liverpool? Martin is one of those who idolised their players in his youth, and Deary and Whitehall have the accents to prove the authenticity of their allegiance. 'I'll be able to go straight to Anfield from home,' says Whitehall. 'The number 59 stops right outside the ground.'

Denis Law could not have raised more laughter. Excited, light-headed laughter, wall-to-wall gags and smiles. And probably happiest of all is Docherty, congratulating and acclaiming all his players.

'Now they are really centre stage and have the opportunity to show what they can do and show how far little old Rochdale have come in the past 12 months. They've all played a part in this and thoroughly deserve to go through.'

While the directors calculate the financial rewards – 'It's got to be six figures and if it's a full house, well' – Docherty decides his players have earned a little treat tonight. He instructs the coach driver to call at Scotch Corner and organises beers and sandwiches all round. A proud, contented mother hen with her chicks would understand how he feels. 'These are great times,' he says, 'the times you hope for.'

But now try telling the players to forget about Liverpool because they have important League matches – against Exeter and Leyton Orient and the like. 'Course I'm not kidding myself they can put it out of their minds totally. But they are pros and promotion is a realistic target for this club. Winning the Cup? Come on. In any case, I can work it in my favour. They are playing for their places at Anfield so I am almost certain I'll get the right response from the players. We've got five games in the League before then and I'll settle for 10 to 12 points from them.'

In the club office, they have to train their thoughts on Liverpool. Tickets to allocate, buses to organise, a windfall to be swept up. Vouchers for Cup tickets will be given on admission to the next home match, on Monday evening. It features Rochdale reserves v Doncaster reserves!

'We expect to get around 5,400 tickets and on past experience it won't be enough,' Les Duckworth says.

'Could be our first 6,000 crowd for a reserve game. Mind you, we've had some great reserve games, you know. Fives and that sort of thing.'

There's a marketing man for you. The commercial brains have come up with the idea of a Cup day breakfast at Spotland as well. 'Strictly limited' tickets at £12.50 will set you up for the trip with a full belly of food and laughs: a fry-up, a comedian and Doc's pre-match views.

Doc and his merry men have one of those rare overnights before the next match, at Exeter. They are back at the Deer Park Hotel, and the manager is having to shuffle his weakened pack. Deary is injured and Gray, who had a double hernia operation during the summer, has been in some discomfort of late and will be rested.

The personnel may change but Rochdale's football at the other St James Park has a familiar, measured look to it. Equally familiar, alas, is the side's lack of penetration and they lose 2–0. Three excursions to the West Country this season have failed to yield a point. 'We had 70 per cent of the game,' pleads Docherty. 'The only disappointing feature was our finishing. Even with half a team we should have got something out of it.'

The Third Division table shows Rochdale in fifth place. The Christmas–New Year period takes on ever greater significance.

The players may be under orders to put Anfield out of their minds but, courtesy of the satellite television age, they have the opportunity to analyse their Cup opponents the following day, in the Premiership encounter with Manchester United. They watch with a mixture of smugness ('We're playing there next month, you know') and trepidation ('If they can do that to United what are

117

they going to do to us?'). Liverpool dispatch a strangely uncommitted United 2–0.

Docherty has tuned in, too. 'I felt like switching off after 10 minutes. Liverpool were terrifying. But, as Alex Ferguson admitted, his team were very poor on the day and if we play the same way, relative to our ability, we'll get exploited tenfold.'

Many doubtless feel they would have been exploited had they turned up for the reserve game to claim a Cup tie voucher and decide to wait until the League match against Preston, on Boxing Day. Nearly 1,300 supporters watched the second team, and were given precisely what Duckworth promised, a five-goal spectacle.

Not so long ago, goals came just as easily to the first team, but another 2–0 defeat, away to modest Orient on a Friday evening, highlights their current plight. So does their League position after the weekend programme has been completed. They are down to sixth. They have a big week coming up: home matches against Preston, the leaders, and neighbouring Bury, another side with aspirations of promotion.

Docherty has his players in for training on Christmas Eve but breaks with football tradition and allows them to stay at home on Christmas Day, even though they have a difficult and important match on Boxing Day.

'They are on trust to behave like professionals and look after themselves,' he explains. 'I've told them to go for a little jog and not over-indulge. As a player I always had to come in for training on Christmas Day and I didn't feel it was necessary. I believe Christmas Day is for the family and that if the players can enjoy the day with their families you will get the right response from them on Boxing Day.'

*　　*　　*

Come the morning of Boxing Day a severe frost is biting into the League programme and the switchboard at Spotland, with Kilpatrick and Morris helping man the phones, is jammed by callers anxious to know if the match is still on. The referee is to inspect the pitch at 11.30. The official, Willie Burns, of Scarborough, takes a look and, hard though it is, decides it is in playable condition. Good news for those who want to clear the festive cobwebs away, and for the club because this all-ticket match means a good pay day. Prices have been put up by £2 'for ground improvement' A cold but sunlit day bristles with anticipation. Foreign players find the Christmas schedule a culture shock yet soon discover why it is a cherished custom.

At around 1.45, supporters still to leave home or travelling to the ground are aghast to hear Rochdale v Preston added to the latest list of postponements read out on the radio. At the ground, disappointment swiftly turns to frustration and anger.

'I want my money back. They've bloody cocked it up again,' says one disgruntled fan heading in the direction of the office.

Inside Spotland, emotions are running just as high. Rochdale officials are furious, claiming the referee changed his mind under pressure from the Preston manager, Gary Peters. Docherty confirms he joined Burns and Peters for a second inspection and, despite his words of indignation, the body language indicates he is not surprised by the revised verdict. What rankles is the sense of an opportunity lost.

He says: 'The pitch is no worse now than it was the first time the referee looked at it. In fact, it's probably better because part of it has been helped by the sun, although the nearside is still hard. Gary said it was too dangerous, that somebody could break a leg, get a bad injury. I said I was prepared to play. Yeah, it was going to be a lottery, but I'm thinking "They don't fancy it – one defeat, flying high, they don't want to risk this". It's psychological, isn't it? They don't fancy it, we do. We're all up for it. But in the end I said, "It's up to you, ref." He then says "It's off". It's a big disappointment for us and all the fans. Look at them.'

Docherty joins some of them, out in the sunshine, offering consolation and explanation. At the secretary's window Karen Smyth patiently deals with the refund demands. Behind her, other club officials and directors are seething over the chaos and cost.

'Scrooge' Morris bursts through the door with his heartfelt seasonal message: 'Forty grand that's cost us. We'd have had 6,000 here today.'

Kilpatrick, in a suitably funereal mood, says: 'We never get a Boxing Day game. We've not had one for three years. The pitch can't be any worse than that plastic thing they used to make us play on at their place.'

Whitehall, bag on shoulder, appears in the reception area and the chairman lightens the load: 'Well done, Whitey, you never put a foot wrong.'

Already the player has decided on alternative activity for the afternoon: 'I'll just have to try that whisky, instead.'

He is not the only one around here in need of a drink. The voucher system for the Cup tie has been thrown into disarray and, after pressurised deliberation, the club open the hatch for the sale of tickets.

That leaves them with the headache of working out what to do with £3,000-worth of festive programmes

('We can hardly use them for the rearranged match if it's at Easter,' Walmsley says) and a mountain of food. This should have been a highly profitable day at the club shop, too.

'We've lost out everywhere,' Duckworth says. 'The food, the bar . . . We're left with egg on our faces.'

Not quite. The spirit of Christmas shines through the gloom and they scrape off the egg, parcel up the turkey lunches, the steaks, the pies and the sandwiches, and send them to local homes for the needy. Dale are sending the Football League a letter of complaint about the referee's handling of the situation, stressing the financial consequences and the embarrassment caused.

Kilpatrick says: 'What hacks me off is that people see this as another cock-up by Rochdale Football Club and it's not. This is none of our doing at all. I am fed up to the teeth of people having a go at this club. I'm not having us ridiculed and made the butt of criticism and sarcasm when we've done absolutely nothing wrong. I don't mind taking criticism when we deserve it, but in this case we are not at fault. Nobody is more upset than the directors at this game being called off after all the effort that was put in to getting it on.'

'Scrooge' is more succinct: 'What a bloody disaster.'

Those who can't be bothered to hang around moaning or queueing for Cup tickets head for home, or the pub or anywhere to patch up their wretched day. Police and stewards have their hands full untangling incoming from outgoing traffic, but in the main tempers are now under control. Heads pop out from windows of cars snaking away to give fans travelling in the opposite direction the news. Somehow it seems comforting to be the first to deliver bad tidings. Sorrow shared and all that.

The weather threatens a serious disruption of Rochdale's mid-winter programme. Already there are doubts about Saturday's home match, against Bury, and devising a training schedule will be a test of the management's ingenuity.

DOCHERTY
We're still in the beg, steal or borrow routine as far as training facilities are concerned. We've been going just down the road to Lenny Barn, a pitch the Council let us have gratis, but obviously we've got a problem there when it's rock hard. There's the all-weather pitch at Heywood, but we have to pay for that – £23.50 for half a pitch, £40 for a full pitch. Sometimes, though, it's been that bad even the all-weather pitch has iced over.

One or two schools lend us their gyms and there's an indoor cricket centre not far from here we can use. Sometimes we'll go upstairs in the stand here and organise some circuit training. You just have to improvise when you don't have the facilities of the Man Uniteds, Arsenals, Liverpools and Boltons. It's a case of keeping the players ticking over, making sure they get a good sweat on.

Few are sweating in Rochdale this week and to no one's surprise the match is postponed long before the caterers and programme sellers can move in. The New Year fixture at Wigan – on 2 January – does go ahead and Docherty wishes it hadn't. His team are subjected to their fourth consecutive 2–0 defeat in away matches and have scored one goal, from a penalty, in five. To compound the camp's dismay, Butler is sent off after a second bookable offence and faces another suspension, of two matches.

Docherty now admits what he has felt for a while.

DOCHERTY
Their minds are already at Liverpool and it's shown in our performance here. It's probably the worst since I've been in charge. If we play like that at Anfield we'll get hammered 15–0. Of course everyone is looking forward to Anfield, me included, and I want the lads to enjoy everything about the experience. But the dangers to our League situation are obvious and in a way I'll be glad when the Cup tie is out of the way.

Manager and players put on a more positive show for the media descending on Spotland in the build-up to Anfield. Liverpool, the most successful club in the history of the English game and 11–2 FA Cup favourites, versus Rochdale, out of form, eighth in the Third Division and 2,500–1 for the Cup. The stuff this competition is made of and the stuff that makes this competition the envy of the world. Somewhere, this weekend, there has to be a shock. This might just be the one.

Docherty is inevitably the focus of most television, radio and newspaper attention, and reporters and photographers arriving at Spotland with route-maps. 'Just look this way, Mick. That's it. Smashing. One more. Good. Could we just go over here and get you . . . This is the one. Can you turn your head slightly to the left. That's it. Good. Oh, hang on, other camera . . .'

His father, Tommy, he is reminded, led Manchester United to Wembley triumph over Liverpool in 1977. Mick has his own omen to draw on: 'I went to Anfield in 1981 with Sunderland and we had to win to guarantee staying up. We won 1–0.'

Players with Liverpool connections are next in demand. Deary and Whitehall fill the Red Scouse requirements and Whitehall, the top scorer, reveals he almost played for Liverpool reserves at Anfield but couldn't make it because he had committed himself to trials with Sheffield United. Nice line. And then there's the touching tale of goalkeeper Chris Clarke's courageous recovery from a fractured skull to find himself in the Cup side as replacement for Gray, still troubled by the scar tissue legacy of his operation. Despite this brush with fame, there are no extravagant preparations and no luxurious retreat. Overnights have brought Dale no luck, anyway.

DOCHERTY

The players themselves feel it's in our best interests to make the day as normal as possible. They'll be at home with their families on Friday night. I'll have my son Matthew with me and we'll have a meal and watch a video. The players will do their usual thing on Saturday morning, turn up at Spotland and we'll go to the match as we would to any other. There has been a lot of attention on us and I've lost track of the people I've done interviews with. I was up at 5.30 to do a GMTV piece. It's been nice and the players have enjoyed that side of it, a bit of glamour and recognition.

But now we want to give a good account of ourselves. We were poor at Wigan and, being human, the lads have been playing at Anfield in their minds for the last three weeks. Our League situation has suffered. I've decided we should go there with a positive strategy because if we play with only one striker they'll steamroller us. We need the ball to be held up. We'll probably get steamrollered anyway, but at least we'll try to play. We've got some pride, you know.

And the result?

'I'll take a draw.'

CHAPTER NINE

Sick as Parrots

They have breakfasted well and now the great armada, led by the team bus, heads west. Twenty-three supporters' coaches set out from Spotland, others from various points in and around the town. They join hundreds of cars also bound for Anfield. Some stick with the motorway, while the M62 roadworks-diversions-delays-wise drivers take the old faithful, the East Lancs. Just outside Rochdale they mingle with long-distance Liverpool supporters, and armies of Manchester United and Sunderland fans on their way to Old Trafford. They exchange tribal gestures – mostly friendly – and exercise their tonsils with the first of the day's war cries.

There is something about this day. Yes, it's corny and hackneyed and cliched, but you have to say it: 'The FA Cup is special'. And third-round day? 'That's extra special.' Rochdale supporters understand that now. They are part of it. This is a trip to the seaside in school time and Christmas day rolled into one. Or, as we shall hear a thousand times, it is 'our Wembley'.

They march to the ground, their insides becoming blenders of anticipation, trepidation, pride and awe. They show their respects too, laying scarves at the Hillsborough memorial. However, Anfield is not one of world football's most aesthetically impressive arenas. Its development has been restricted by stereotype rows of football neighbourhood houses and, once inside, many visitors are disappointed. It is not as big as you might imagine, and those tacky, multi-coloured blocks of seating represent one of the less inspired legacies of the stadia revolution. But then people, rather than plastic and concrete, traditionally have been the imposing features here; players and supporters saluted for their presentation and appreciation of the game.

Rochdale's players are conscious of that heritage now, as they file down the tight corridor to the dressing room, as they sift through the match programme, and as they step out on to the pitch for their first feel of Anfield. They gawp around the stands, particularly the fabled Kop end, which surrendered its concrete terracing to plastic seats only a couple of years ago. 'It's great for the players, isn't it?' Docherty reverently whispers. 'I want them to soak up the atmosphere, I want them to take it all in and enjoy every minute of it. Same for the fans. It's a day they should never forget.'

Already the 'normal game' has gone out of the window. The players have been relaxed, the card school has been in full swing, the usual routine has been adhered to. But how can you treat it as Hartlepool or Barnet when John Barnes saunters by dressed as if he has come straight from the set of 'Joseph and His Amazing Technicolor Dreamcoat'?

Someone suggests Rochdale's players ought to be a little more 'sartorially adventurous'. Butler draws attention to a slight hitch: 'We can't afford anything like that on a £50 bonus'.

Docherty placates him: 'If we win I'll speak to the chairman and see if we can sort something out.'

Deary is preoccupied with Liverpool's line-up. He gives earnest consideration to each name on the team-sheet and concludes: 'Rubbish.'

Another voice, anxious lest his colleagues be lured into a longer term sense of security, gives advance warning: 'It gets tougher in the fourth round.'

If they are nervous then this is a pretty good cover-up. Even more convincing is their performance in the opening quarter of the match. They contain Liverpool and, momentarily at least, have central defenders Mark Wright and John Scales floundering. Then Robbie Fowler, with a shot across Clarke, registers his 21st goal of the season and the travelling hordes wonder if their team will now fold. Not a bit of it. They retaliate and Whitehall and Thompson require the goalkeeper, David James, to stretch his considerable frame.

Alas, with half-time and thunderous appreciation looming, the fantasy shatters. Stan Collymore, at £8.5m the most expensive player in the land and probably banking more than enough to buy Spotland, speculates with a low effort that ought to yield nothing yet manages to elude Clarke. More dividends are rattling into his account. Before half-time, Collymore and Liverpool have another. The walk back to the dressing room is the procession of the stunned.

Docherty accepts the game is up but urges his men to salvage something. Enjoyment, for instance. And the subs need not feel out of it. They will be given the opportunity to join in the fun. The faces betray no sign of terror, but the expressions indicate scant anticipation of carefree recreation.

For all the manager's valiant endeavours, any prospect of enjoyment or indeed any other form of consolation is swiftly dashed. Within 3 minutes of the resumption, Valentine turns Jason McAteer's cross into his own goal. After 61 minutes, Dale concede a fifth, although the goal does secure them a place in the annals of the game. It is scored by the substitute, Ian Rush, and is his 42nd in the FA Cup, overtaking the record for the competition previously held by Denis Law.

Collymore completes his hat trick with more than 20 minutes remaining and Docherty is squirming on the bench. Defeat is one thing but annihilation quite another. 3, 4–0, say, would not have been so bad. You can live with that. It is Anfield, after all. Here we are, though, at 6–0 and Liverpool have the time and appetite to gobble up loads more. The pain is almost too much to bear.

There is compassion in the air after all. A combination of stoic resistance by Clarke and his colleagues at the back, and somewhat diluted concern in the home ranks confine Liverpool to only one more goal, smacked in by McAteer after 84 minutes. Modern Dale have at least spared themselves the ignominy of another entry in the record books. Eight goals remains the biggest losing margin suffered by the club.

Docherty and his men summon the decency if barely the enthusiasm to applaud their fans, probably wondering when or if they will ever see most of them again. The players' expressions, as they turn back towards the tunnel, reveal some of their inner feelings. This was not the way they had envisaged their famous day unfolding. All right, so they are not surprised they have lost. But 7–0!

The manager, although fumbling for his stick-on smile, musters a brave face for the media. Here, too, he is entering unfamiliar territory – a Press room, rather than any available wall space in a corridor. He impresses the national boys with his candour and his appreciation of Rush.

'He has been a shining light to all professionals. His work-rate, application and goalscoring ability have been tremendous examples for everyone in the game,' the Doc says. 'I made a point of shaking hands with each and every one of my players after the game. They did their best and it has been a great experience for them, playing at a wonderful stadium against one of the world's best club teams. Next week we're back to reality – against Darlington.'

That goes down well. He leaves the pack with a nice quote and seeks out the soothing embrace of the 'upstairs' hospitality. The players, meanwhile, ferret around for anything they can retrieve from the day – Liverpool kit, autographs, handshakes. For an hour and a half they were on the same pitch, their paths permitted to cross by the freakish powers of the FA Cup, and now they are on different planes again. The Rochdale players acknowledge their place without embarrassment or resentment. This is the way it is.

Martin presses his face against a trophy cabinet like a child peering into a sweet shop. 'You see them on TV and think they are good,' he says, 'but playing against them is just unbelievable. They had us chasing shadows. They pass it about nice and slow, see an opening, then bang, bang and it's in the net. John Barnes gets slated by a lot of fans in this country, but they want to try to get near him and take the ball off him. It's just impossible.'

The reward Rochdale were guaranteed will come in an envelope rather than a glass case, although the cheque is also going to fall short of expectations. The attendance of 28,126 is 7,000 to 8,000 down on the figure the visiting party had hoped for and a sign that the economic recovery may have by-passed Merseyside. Dale's directors (minus Kilpatrick, who is on a long-planned trip to South Africa) reckon they still should be due a pay-out of around £125,000. All in all, perhaps not such a bad day. For the bank manager.

Come mid-evening the money, the experience, the generous reception and the sympathetic hearing matter not one jot to Docherty. He is inconsolable. As if to rub salt in the wound, Dale's great crusade merits a mere fleeting clip on *Match of the Day*, and that to acclaim Rush's goalscoring landmark. Rochdale, the focus of all that attention in the previous week, are now discarded without so much as a backward glance. This, too, is the way it is.

Docherty has had more than he can take. Like most wounded creatures, he prefers to suffer in silence and solitude. He unplugs the telephone and curls up in his lair for the weekend.

DOCHERTY
I wanted my own company. I'd had enough and didn't want to talk to anyone. I'm gutted. Perhaps I shouldn't be and I know you have to be realistic about these things. But we didn't do ourselves justice, we all know we didn't, and by the end of the day I couldn't be doing with anything or anybody, you know? You try to take all the pressure, absorb it and take the weight off the players. You try to put on a bold front because that's part of the job. It's what's expected. But we're all human and we

can all find it too much sometimes. It's all just got to me.

The thing was, we'd done quite well up to three minutes from half-time and if we'd gone in at half-time still 1–0 we'd have been really up for the second half. But then they get two in 45 seconds and the game was over. When the lads came in, you could see they were out of it and it was very difficult to pick them up. So you accept you're not going to win but still try to get something from the second half and enjoy the experience. Instead, they just hammered us.

It was terrible watching it. At 6–0 and with 20 minutes to go I was praying they wouldn't get double figures. Dear God, I thought, please don't let that happen. I couldn't have taken that. Fortunately, the lads dug in again and we got away with seven. Now I've got to pick myself up and pick the players up. It's got to be done and it's down to me.

Most managers – indeed most professional men, for that matter – will tell you they lean heavily on patient and for-giving wives. Docherty's marriage broke down 16 months ago, no longer able to withstand a strain exerted by the job and its social requirements.

DOCHERTY
Eventually, I suppose, I paid the price for being a football manager. You know what it's like. You're working long hours, all hours, and even after the match it's not over. You have a drink with the other manager, officials, the board, guests, and in the end I've got to be honest and admit, it was the drink. She

couldn't cope with it any more. I asked her to come along and get involved, but she didn't want to know. I had my responsibility to the job. All managers do.

It was very hard for a year or so but I'm settling down now. I've got my own place and we're still friends. Our two daughters are grown up but with Matthew being only 13, that obviously made things difficult.

Monday morning after the Saturday before, the ham and the psychologist in Docherty rise to the challenge of entertaining and reviving the morale of his adopted 'family'. He pushes them through a vigorous, muscle-straining, hard-running training session – and then takes them off to a local pub for their Christmas party. The timing may be unconventional – this is 8 January, remember – but it could not have been better. If they were still feeling sorry for themselves before the first medicinal application, their spirits are suitably restored long before the last of them vacates the premises. That is believed to be about 4 o'clock on a sobering Tuesday morning, but the precise details, you will understand, are fuzzy around the edges.

The real world, for all the players, comes zooming into focus just hours later. The next phase of Doc's remedy is another pounding training session. The cobwebs are blown away all right. And much more besides. One by one, half a dozen of them slink away and throw up.

DOCHERTY
It's the best thing we could have done after Liverpool. We all thrashed out what happened at Anfield. Everyone had his say and soon the strength of the team, and their team spirit, showed through.

They've trained hard again, and suffered, but they pushed themselves through it and now they are ready to get back to the business of the League. Darlington is our big match now – it's everything as far as we are concerned. Win this and we're on our way again. I think we need to win 11 more games. I'm still confident we can make the play-offs.

A merciful day off on Wednesday and vomit-free training on Thursday bring the first-team players to a treat of final preparations for the visit of Darlington. Hornets, winding down their season earlier than in the past because of the advent of summer rugby league this year, have granted their housemates permission to use Spotland once a week for training.

Docherty says: 'They've only one match left, although they could have more with a good Cup run, but anyway, we've come to this arrangement and it's a timely bonus for us. We can get in some good work on set pieces on a good pitch and really get ourselves ready for tomorrow.'

While the first team luxuriate, the stiffs are consigned to the quaintly named Lenny Barn playing field. It is conveniently situated, just down the hill from Spotland, and, better still, comes at a good price. Nothing. But a rubbish pitch by any other name, in any place, and at any cost is still a rubbish pitch. And Lenny Barn is a rubbish pitch. You will stumble upon it – literally, if you are not careful – at the bottom of a field which slopes down from a school. It looks like a school pitch, the bumpy type you dreaded playing on because it always gave the home team an unfair advantage. The contours would provide useful study material for a geography class at the other end of the field. No wonder Docherty is salivating at the prospect of training at Spotland. Jimmy Robson has the dubious honour of presiding here. 'Come to see how the other half lives, have you?' he asks.

This is living? Well, for these players it is a way of making a living and they are grateful for it. They could be on a factory floor, on a production line, or down a pit. This workforce, especially the younger members, believe they will progress to smoother pitches and grander stages. On this fresh, invigorating morning they adhere to the unofficial club motto: Just Get On With It.

Five of them jog round the pitch, then form a tight circle for stretching exercises and a good chinwag. They catch up on the latest movements of other players and are unanimous in condemning the dismissal of Newcastle's David Ginola at Arsenal the other night. The first booking was a diabolical decision, they agree. As well as the referee, the commentator also comes in for a slagging. Normal football chatter, then.

Robson engages the two goalkeepers in catching practice, while the rest, in another, larger circle, are endeavouring to play first-time passes as well as cut out the two pigs in the middle. Try that on a cheese-grater of a surface. And here's a turn-up. This absorbing performance is being orchestrated by none other than Big Willo.

Robson is still in charge here, calling all the players together and sorting out two sides for a game. As they line up, the bibs and the plains, a familiar chunky, balding but displaced figure takes his position in one of the attacks. Andy Ritchie, once of Manchester United, more recently of Oldham Athletic, is rumoured to be at odds with his new club, Scarborough, and now he appears training with Dale. You can be sure that this will be on the local bush radio in no time.

A few pupils, on mid-morning break, drift down from the school to watch. More, however, prefer to indulge themselves in their own game. Most of these youngsters are Asians and their enthusiastic activity serves as a reminder of untapped potential, not only in this town but in many urban areas throughout the country. The obligatory man and his dog materialise on the far touchline, pause briefly, and move on.

Ritchie's neat control, turn and strike are at least appreciated by the other players. No mean feat on this pitch. Robson is less impressed when someone dallies too long on the ball. 'Pass it, pass it,' the doyen orders. The young man passes it.

Robson halts proceedings after 20 minutes or so and organises shooting practice. He lays off the ball and a player runs on and shoots. The two goalkeepers take turns in the firing line, each encouraging the other in compliance with the unwritten rules of the keepers union. The encouragement for the outfield players is of a purely selfish nature. If they miss the target the ball goes down a steep bank and miles across another field and they have to retrieve it. Oh, doesn't it take you back?

'You need some fielders, Jimmy,' one of the keepers mocks as another shot flies in the direction of Blackburn.

This, it now transpires, has been the half-time entertainment. The match resumes and Ritchie wishes it hadn't. Urged to 'hold' by Big Willo, Ritchie is a helpless bystander as the ball bobbles up in the air in a manner that would have defied Pele's control. Big Willo is soon shouting again, this time chastising a team-mate as another move breaks down. Before it can get too heated, Robson announces the end of training. The YTS boys collect the balls, the older players get into the cars and drive back up the hill to Spotland to shower and change.

Already the first-team players are cleaning themselves up and Docherty is jauntily content with the morning's work. 'Yeah, we've had a good session on set pieces. It's smashing to be able to do it on here.'

Docherty is explaining that Formby will miss tomorrow's match when Dawson brings him a medical update: 'Doc Mace says he'll give him an injection if you want, but I've told him we don't want to do that.'

The manager concurs. He also gives nodding acknowledgement of his interest in Ritchie. 'At the moment I've just given him permission to train with us because he still lives near here and it's obviously convenient. He's still got it, I know that. Don't worry, I'm keeping tabs on the situation.'

Docherty is keeping tabs on the progress of another injured player, too, and scurries along the corridor with massaging words: 'If it's still coming along all right let's look at giving it 45 minutes with the reserves, in 10 days' time. No physical stuff, just a work-out. Do you good.'

The player nods his thanks. So does yet another as the Doc brandishes a pay packet. 'Heavy one this. Must be yours.'

Can this be the same man? The man so 'gutted' he locked himself away from the outside world a few days ago? In an instant he is back at the other end of the corridor, pursued by Big Willo. Seems the striker may soon be going out in a loan deal.

Karen Smyth appears outside the dressing room and sheepishly knocks on the door. As it is opened she covers her eyes and shields her embarrassment with her hands, and calls to a player that he is wanted on the telephone, all to the accompaniment of predictable ribbing. Message delivered, she quickly retreats, followed by a player with a towel discreetly wrapped around him.

Other players are now dressed, heading for home. Deary and Thompson leave together, two experienced professionals comfortable in the routine of Third Division football again after the misadventure of Anfield.

DEARY
When I think about it now, the disappointing part was that we kept giving the ball back to them as soon as we got it. I wasn't disappointed with the way they played because I knew they were going to play like that. I don't think the scoreline flattered them. They deserved it. We didn't really play.

I didn't enjoy the second half one bit because they absolutely slaughtered us. But it's not affected me at all because I half expected it. Not 7–0, but the way they're playing at the moment I think they are the best team in the country.

Thompson is equally candid about the experience.

THOMPSON
I think when you are 1–0 down after 43 minutes and go 3–0 down at half-time it shows a lack of professionalism. Losing another goal, straight after half-time, was the same. If we hadn't done that I think it would have been three or four rather than seven. I think seven, in any standard of football, is embarrassing.

In some ways the Liverpool tie might have been preying on people's minds before we went there.

Since we beat Darlington to go through, we haven't won a game. It's ironic we've got Darlington again tomorrow. We have had the Indian sign over them so far this year, so confidence should be quite high that we can beat them again.

That mood was coaxed back, they confirm, by events earlier in the week. 'The Christmas do was good for team spirit. Everyone stuck together and everyone loved it. Then on Tuesday we did some more running and no, I wasn't sick,' said Deary.

'I was, but then if you put your work in during training you should be sick now and then!' added Thompson.

'I felt dizzy,' conceded Deary. 'But I mean, it's been a hard week and I think we needed it to get back to basics, back down to hard work. Now we can concentrate on the task we've got ahead of us, and I don't think it should be a hard task to make the play-offs. I think we should be looking more at getting one of those three places for automatic promotion. We'll know better over the next two or three games. If we do well, we can set our sights higher again.'

CHAPTER TEN

Home Truths

Perhaps this is what they mean by the magic of the Cup – one week you have a following of 5,500, the next 1,945. The Cup giveth and the Cup taketh away. There is nothing magical, mystical or even vaguely memorable about this League match against Darlington at Spotland. It is an unceremonious return to reality and time to face up to some home truths. Despite a first-half lead, courtesy of Steve Whitehall's penalty, Rochdale are beaten 2–1. The rumbling message from the diehards is unequivocal: 'Pathetic.'

The pained expressions among players, management and directors convey total agreement. A team that delivered as regularly as the milkman seems to have forgotten the route. They last scored a goal in open play more than two months ago and are now leaking them with alarming regularity. Jason Peake's game is disintegrating, the defence quakes under pressure and Chris Clarke, still in goal for Ian Gray, appears incapable of inspiring confidence in those around him. The consequence of this sorry state of affairs is that Dale are now 10th in the Third Division.

'We were very poor,' Docherty concedes. 'It's particularly disappointing to lose at home because if we're going to keep up a promotion challenge we have to maintain our form here. There's no doubt that if your goalkeeper is struggling it's going to affect the confidence of those in front of him. Gray has had a scan and we'll get the results in a day or two. The scar tissue from his hernia op is troubling him and if he can't play for a while we may try to get a keeper in on loan.'

At times like this, when results are going against you and the natives are growing restless, a manager must be seen to be active and Docherty lets it be known he is 'ducking and diving' in an effort to strengthen his squad. One player unlikely to join the club, however, is Andy Ritchie, the 35-year-old striker that Scarborough, apparently, are prepared to release.

DOCHERTY
It's all right being able to sign a player, even on a free, but it's not as simple, or cheap, as that. He wants £750 a week, a £15,000 signing-on fee – and a car! There's no way this club is going to go along with demands like that. When I quit playing and went into coaching I took an 80 per cent cut in my £300 a week wages because the opportunity was there to try and build something for the future.

Having said that, the teams we are trying to compete against are spending money, big money. Even Bury are. I also realise Preston and Gillingham get the crowds and ours this weekend . . . Well, I'm not surprised. I'm afraid it's typical. But as I've said to the directors, my worry is that unless we do spend something it could all go down the Swanee.

We're back in the same old predicament, and I can see both sides of the argument. I have to be sensible and reasonable, but that can be hard. I just don't want to see it all go wrong. You know there are going to be ups and downs and a manager, like anyone else, needs a pat on the back every now and then. One thing's for sure, he'll get stick when things aren't going well. I go through my blue periods and go away to hide for a while, but I never let them *see* me down and, with or without money to spend, I'll be up front, trying to sort it.

What I'm thinking now is that perhaps it's time to give youth a chance. I've got to freshen things up. We're beginning to look a bit too creaky and vulnerable. Maybe some younger legs would help.

Much younger legs are trampling all over a couple of school pitches in Rochdale's cause the following morning. The club's Centre of Excellence teams are playing their counterparts from Manchester United. The under-15s and under-13s are away, the under-16s and under-14s are at home, which is in the Castleton district of the town, and even at this level the gulf between the clubs stretches beyond the range of the naked eye.

Rochdale's youngsters kick-in, watched by parents hugging flasks and fending off players' already bored siblings, while United's latest protégés ape their famous seniors with a warm-up routine of stretches and exercises. The mimicry goes on during the match. A tiny bundle of mischief with cherubic features in the under-14s team pours out a repertoire of flicks and dinks and postures. Wonder where he learned all that? One of the coaches suspects he knows. 'Is that your Cantona?' he calls.

The goals flow just as readily from the red-shirted youngsters in this game of three thirds, but the Rochdale coach sustains his enthusiastic entreaties all through the 10–0 defeat and his players do not appear to be mentally scarred for life.

Keeping an eye on each match are Rochdale director Rod Brierley and the club's elder statesman, vice-president and office factotum, Tom Nichol. All part of the responsibility of being involved. Shouldering responsibility for the under-16s affairs is Dave Bywater. His obvious interest in the goalkeeper is soon explained – this is his son, Stephen. At the age of 14 he is a comparative baby in this company, but he has the self-confidence of a veteran and his promise has been recognised by a call-up for a North of England representative side.

The son and grandson of goalkeepers, he has ample opportunity to demonstrate that the family tradition and pride are in safe hands. Father drools from the top touchline as mother and sister look on from the bottom touchline. 'We all like to get involved,' Dave says as he scurries by, following play to the other end.

Play is mostly at Stephen's end in this orthodox game of two halves. A number of Rochdale's players will be considered for the YTS scheme but already United's boys are a class apart.

'We know that, and you can't expect anything else,' Bywater says. 'They have players from all over the country and Ireland. Ours are basically local lads. See that lad over there, and this one here – England schoolboy internationals. We can't compete against Man United at any level, but we do the best we can and try to impress upon lads that they are more likely to get a chance with a club like Rochdale. But if United invite a young lad along, what is he going to say?'

Recently United have been in bother with the authorities over the 'poaching' of young players and, right on cue, a youngster in a red shirt, ambling along the touchline, sheepishly says 'hello' to Bywater.

'Case in point,' Bywater says. 'He was one of our lads. Got the chance to go to United, off he went. That's what we're up against.'

His under-16s are up against it by half-time. They trail 3–0 and Bywater applies soothing words. United's coach, who bombarded his charges with instructions through the first half, now tells them: 'I'm not changing it yet because you're playing so well, especially as the surface is crap.'

Both coaches ring the changes in the second half, Bywater explaining that all 16 members of the squad are promised an active part. The pattern of the game, however, is the same and United rattle in four more goals. One of the players identified as a schoolboy international tumbles dramatically as he bears down on Dale's penalty area, incurring the displeasure of Bywater, who scorns: 'He's diving for fun.'

The player throws back a contemptuous look and an accompanying curse. An indignant Bywater marches to the United coach and reports the affront. Moments later the player is withdrawn and taken for an educational stroll, the coach's arm around him and words in his ear.

At the end, as Bywater calls his squad together for a debrief, the chastised United player threads his way through them – much as he had done in the match – and apologises. The matter is closed to Bywater's satisfaction and he tells his youngsters: 'Don't be disheartened, don't be down. They've got players from all over the country. And Ireland . . .'

They are dispatched to the extremities of the pitch to take down the nets and collect the corner flags, and Bywater says: 'It's obviously difficult for them when they play the likes of United, but we do have our better days, against the Burys and Wigans. Today they've had to experience what the seniors went through at Anfield.'

Surely, though, Rochdale should be tapping that well of Asian potential we saw at the school near Lenny Barn and can see at many schools and playing fields in the borough? 'We've tried,' Bywater replies. 'Keith Hicks goes round the schools, inviting them to the Centre of Excellence. They say they'll come along, but they don't. They just play among themselves. It's strange and very frustrating.'

Those who did come along are now making for the refuge of the dressing room and refreshments, dispensed by Mrs Bywater. 'Come and have a nice cup of tea,' Dave beckons.

More problems beckon for Docherty. Butler and Deary will miss the match at Cardiff because of suspension and, although Gray could be risked, the manager is reluctant to take that step. The day before the trip Thackeray dislocates a shoulder in a freak training accident – at dreaded Lenny Barn. The return of Stuart at least increases the team's creativity count.

Chances are duly created and almost routinely spurned. Then, 10 minutes from the end, Clarke hands Cardiff a winner. Dale are down to 12th and the local paper, billowing with souvenir Anfield pictures a fortnight ago, now runs a critical comment piece under the headline: 'Happy? Not one bit we're not!'

Docherty, having manoeuvred Big Willo to Chester-field on loan, is gratified to hear the striker scored in his first reserve game. He has another match to sell himself to the Derbyshire club and enhance Dale's prospects of bringing in another player. In the meantime Docherty has to pick a side for the match at Scarborough, and he decides Gray must play.

'Overall Chris had his best game for a while,' Docherty says, 'but his error cost us a goal and the game. Sod's Law. I can't get anyone on loan before this game so I'm throwing Ian in. He's got to play through the pain barrier. He isn't the first and he won't be the last. I need him. Just being there will give the defence so much more confidence.'

It appears to have revived the Doc's confidence, too. Another match, another target. Win this – Scarbrough are, after all, next to bottom – and win on Saturday at home to Torquay – they are, after all, bottom – and we're back on the rails. The players are more subdued. The video player is idle and silent. 'Yeah,' Docherty says. 'Probably pensive. They know how important it is. We've got to be positive and go for a win.'

He and the directors are going prepared for a cold night. Rod Brierley shudders at the thought of 'that cold, open stand'. Michael Mace, pulling a woolly hat from his pocket, reckons Scarborough's ground is 'the coldest in the country'.

Ah, but doesn't someone always have a *colder* story to tell? The Doc does. He recalls a youth match at Burnley's notoriously exposed training ground. Playing at right back, he looked ahead for his right-winger only to see his colleague, arms rigid by his side, wander off the pitch like some programmed zombie, over a bridge and on towards the dressing room. 'It was that cold he had hypothermia. Frozen stiff he was. He got in a hot bath and took forever to thaw out.'

Jimmy Robson remembers the days when they had a simple solution to frozen and snowbound pitches – they played on them. The groundsmen coloured the lines and they got on with it. One over-resourceful groundsman daubed blue paint on the goalposts and bar, but he was told such ingenuity could not be permitted and had to scrub them white again.

John Dawson enters the spirit of the season with an update on rehearsals for the panto coming soon to his local church hall. The Doc is relieved to hear his jolly Thespian physio has been excused the Saturday matinee performance of Simple Simon. Don't tell us which role you're playing, John . . . 'I'm Simple Simon.'

The players are now restless for a little entertainment and a YTS player, James Price, summoned for his debut at the age of 17, ventures down the bus and reaches for the platter of sandwiches, which everyone but the new boy knows are out of bounds until after the match.

'Where are you going with them?' the Doc growls.

'Back there,' says the new boy.

'Put them back. I think somebody's set you up, son.'

The new boy slinks back to his place among the sniggering elders and Docherty shakes his patriarchal head. All part of the initiation process. Not that the manager is concerned young Price will be too wet behind the ears when he takes up his duties at left-back. 'He's a good tackler. He'll be fine.'

They arrive at Scarborough's ground little more than an hour before the kick-off and if there is a sea out there they don't see it. The night is black and the wind has the cutting edge of a sabre. Docherty takes the reflex stroll onto the pitch, which is bumpy but not frozen. He scans the surface, then faces the gale. 'This is a night to find out who wants it,' he declares.

Back in the dressing room, Whitehall wants nail-clippers. He can't find them in Dawson's orange box because cunning John, intent on outwitting the phantom nailclipper lifter, has put them in his green box. Offending nail duly clipped, Whitey is in a quandary. 'Now, John, shall I put them in the green box or the orange box?' John points to the green but fears his cover is blown. 'I won't tell anyone,' Whitey assures him. 'Actually, I've put them in the teapot.'

John is much in demand before the match for massages. A cold night can wreak havoc with muscles. The players peer into the kit box at the options. 'Short sleeves, yeah,' laughs one. Another returns from his Siberian recce with the verdict: 'No point staying out there any longer. You'll never warm up tonight.'

They raise their body temperatures with verbals, pumping each other up as kick-off approaches. All have good luck messages for the new boy and Docherty tells him: 'Enjoy it. Don't worry about making a mistake. I made one once – 1968, I think it was.'

General instructions include 'Get it in the mixer', which translates to 'Plenty of service into the penalty area'. The two wide men, Thompson and Stuart, are told to use the width yet also be prepared to tuck in. 'Peakey, you don't always have to be pinpoint. Play searching balls as well.'

Peakey is receptive and delivers his own demand as they filter through the dressing room door to a rush of psyche. 'Come on. Twelfth position! That's an insult. We're better than that.'

Rochdale kick into the icy blast and Docherty, hunched in his many layers and the Perspex shelter, needs only 30 seconds to capture the scenario: 'Bumpy pitch, freezing cold, howling wind – bloody great, heh?'

Despite the elements, Dale muster one or two early threats and Stuart has a couple of shots blocked by Scarborough's goalkeeper. By and large, however, the visitors are under siege and taking a fearful pounding from Scarborough's centre-forward, Neil Trebble. He is tall and not surprisingly a problem in the air. But to the Doc's dismay, he is deft on the deck, too. Just what you need when Butler is missing!

Thompstone, one of the substitutes, provides some intelligence on Scarborough's 'agent provocateur' as Valentine and Bayliss again scamper to cover. 'They bought him out of the Army. He's ex-Scunthorpe and Preston.'

Docherty is thankful he has Gray back even if the keeper is uncharacteristically reluctant to come for crosses. 'You can see the difference he makes, though,' Thompstone says, leaning over towards his manager. 'You can see the difference in the lads' confidence.'

They are relieved to retreat to the dressing room at half-time for a cup of hot tea, still at 0–0. With the wind behind them in the second half, they feel they can change the course of the match and plunder that elusive win. 'Don't be afraid to shoot from distance,' Docherty urges. 'Because there will be mistakes, a bobble off the keeper, anything. This is a night for an own goal.'

Robson, having had the benefit of a more elevated position in the stand, adds his observations on strategy, positional play and movement, and they trot out again to put the wind up Scarborough. Wouldn't you know it? The wind has dropped. Docherty, settling on the bench with

Dawson and his substitutes, grunts and throws his eyes to the heavens. Just like Carlisle last year, he is reminded. Scarborough's number 11 still feels it is cold enough for gloves. 'You tart,' Thompstone mocks.

Docherty is soon on his feet bellowing at his players. 'Stick it . . . get it over the top,' is the recurring theme. It has scant effect and, to no one's amazement, Trebble puts the home side ahead midway through the half. If Docherty turns and looks up to the directors' box, he will see the scowls on the faces of Kilpatrick and company. He doesn't, and three minutes later he watches with gratification as his team work the ball in from the left and Peake, the one player on the night who looks remotely like a player, strikes a sweet equaliser with his left foot.

Had Whitehall any confidence in his right foot, even as a 'swinger', he might score another for Dale, but he drags the ball to his left side and the chance evaporates. Scarborough bring on the unsettled Ritchie and at the end Dale are thankful to hang on for a point. A clutch of travelling fans among the small crowd – officially given as a suspiciously round 1400 – applaud the players before setting off on the long drive back home. Some of them, stuck in traffic in Leeds, did not arrive until half-time, and you wonder whether you should be filled with admiration – or sympathy.

Price, who has a booking as a personal memento of the occasion, receives the congratulations of his colleagues as they shuffle back into the dressing room. 'Great debut,' they chorus. Docherty singles out the new boy for a personal word of praise and has a positive dictum for the rest: 'Lots of effort, pleased with the way you got back and you've stopped the rot . . .'

You just know when there's a 'but' coming, don't you? And sure enough . . .

'But can anyone explain to me why they got all that space to score their goal?'

Valentine throws up a hand. 'I can.' He argues that their area marking system dictated he had to challenge for the header, which left the big man free. The header proved indecisive, the big man wasn't. The Doc nods ruefully.

In the boardroom, the Rochdale contingent can barely contain their agitation. Stopping the rot with a scrambled draw is not their idea of mission accomplished. 'Garbage,' Kilpatrick pronounces. 'Complete and utter garbage, right through the team.'

Brierley's contorted expression confirms his agreement. And just in case anyone missed the point, Kilpatrick adds: 'I mean . . . there was just nothing. Nothing. It was an awful, awful game.'

He is interrupted by a series of presentations, all of which seem to involve the ubiquitous Trebble. If he is not receiving awards for man of the match he is presenting them to the shirt sponsors, the match ball sponsor, the wind of one half sponsor . . .

'We could do with someone like him,' Kilpatrick whispers. 'We had nothing up front tonight.'

Docherty would doubtless welcome Trebble in his attack. Shaw was anonymous this evening and Whitehall a trifle better. Like many goalscorers, Whitehall probes the extremes of emotions. When they are going in, earning bonuses for the whole team and points for the club, he is the main man. When they are not going in, he is the villain of the piece: selfish, can't play with others, undependable. Such accusations are even more likely when the player in question is on a £1,000 bonus for scoring 20 goals in the season and currently has 17. What's more, he is pigeon-holed as a Scouser: bubbly and mischievous, with plenty to say for himself and the others besides. Again, when the goals are going in, that makes him a character and great for team spirit. When they are not, he is a pain in the posterior.

Back on the coach, Kilpatrick calls Docherty to his front seat for the kind of chat you try to avoid with your employer, bank manager, or mother-in-law. At the back, the card school is in session and, judging from the sounds, Whitehall is having more success than he had at the McCain Stadium. He quits while he's ahead, but then this pigeon-holed Scouser is nobody's fool. How many footballers nominate as their favourite TV programme *Fifteen-to-One*, that quick-fire test of knowledge and nerve? There again, how many footballers took up the game at the age of 17?

WHITEHALL
I played at primary school, but my secondary school was at St Anselm's College in Birkenhead, and they didn't play football. You weren't even allowed to play football in the yard. It was a rugby and cross-country school, so I was in the cross-country team and I got into the rugby first XV. I also captained the cricket first XI.

I got a Saturday job at the time and started playing football on a Sunday afternoon. It was a case of 'as luck would have it'. The fellow who lived next door to us ran a Sunday side and I just happened to get with him. I played for his side and it all snow-balled from there. At 18 I was playing in the West Cheshire League and got a letter from Tranmere

153

Rovers, asking me to play for their reserves. But the club had financial problems; Frank Worthington, the manager, was kicked out and I got a letter saying 'thanks but no thanks' along with others in the reserves. After a while, Southport came in for me.

It was during his spell with Southport that he almost played for Liverpool reserves. Anfield's playing resources had been stretched by commitments elsewhere, and Southport made some of their likelier lads available to get Liverpool through a second-team fixture. Whitehall, however, was due at Sheffield United the following day for a trial and forbidden from turning out at Anfield. Since a career at Bramall Lane failed to materialise it was a particularly frustrating miss.

Whitehall was a semi-professional at Southport. His day job was in the Civil Service, working with the Land Registry and Charities Commission, where he became an executive officer. And then, in the 1991–92 season, he was offered the chance to become a full-time professional footballer – at Rochdale. Not Liverpool or Manchester United or even Sheffield United. But Rochdale. He took it.

WHITEHALL
The Civil Service was a job for life, so in terms of long-term security it was a gamble. I also took a cut in wages to come to Rochdale because I had some football money as well as my wage before. But it's still a dream, isn't it, playing professional football? Not many people get the chance to do it, at whatever level, and I did. Given the chance, you've got to go for it, haven't you?

People come in and out of football and, especially

154

on the non-League scene, you do hear of people getting one- or two-year contracts with League clubs and that's it, they come back again. If that had happened to me it would have been a bad situation because I would have struggled to get another job.

Whitehall – dark, 5'9", lean – believes even at the age of 29 he has not made up for time lost.

WHITEHALL
I missed out on important experience by not playing between 11 and 17. Even now I struggle in certain situations. I will still want to go and score a goal if we're 1–0 up with 10 minutes to go, but you don't do that as a professional footballer, you keep hold of the ball.

I think everyone has aspirations of getting higher, but if you can't enjoy being a professional footballer, even in a game like tonight's, then there is something wrong with you. I've had the rest of the day off before the game today, I've gone up there, I've played the game, and I've been paid for it. If I was still working in the Civil Service there's a good chance I'd still have been playing for Southport, perhaps on some ground not as good as that.

[Not that Whitehall is idle for much of his spare time. He is laying foundations for his future.] I'm in my second year at Salford University, doing a physiotherapy degree run by the PFA, so there is stuff in the pipeline. I've already got a biology degree so it's based on my previous education. I go after training on Mondays and Thursdays, which means they are long days, especially as I live in

Liverpool. I get home about half past eight in the evening. At the moment I'm also doing clinical practice in a hospital on my days off. With the course and a couple of young kids I've got my hands full. I used to play golf and go fishing but both have just about been knocked on the head because I haven't got the time.

Sometimes I'll bring my books with me to read on the away trips, especially the longer ones. I don't always play cards but I'll maybe make up the numbers on the way back. I did tonight and it's paid off. I'm loaded! I sometimes wonder what other players do with their time. A lot of the lads who have come in at 16 have got used to having the afternoons off, going to bed for a couple of hours and doing nothing. They tend to get a bit lazy.

But more and more the PFA are getting into the lads, explaining what's going on and encouraging them to get on courses. Graham Shaw there is doing a degree in law, Mark Stuart's doing some sort of computer course and Jason Peake's looking at some literature they've given him. John Deary's got himself in business with his brother, I think, doing double glazing. More and more of the lads are sorting out a second career, or something to fall back on when their football has finished. They also get more involved in the community, coaching kids in the schools, that sort of thing.

[Injury can hasten the necessity of that fall-back career, but Whitehall maintains the threat does not haunt him.] That's something you don't worry about, really, even playing up front. If you started worrying about things like that you'd put yourself off your game. You'd pull out of tackles and that's when you start getting injured, so you're best off not thinking about it at all. The new instructions to referees about tackling from behind have improved things for forwards, but to be honest it's never been anything compared with playing in the Birkenhead Sunday League!

Whenever retirement comes for these players, they won't have the riches of the stars to live off. While the top Premiership players pull in their thousands – in some cases many thousands – of pounds a week, land multi-million pound boot deals, live in mansions and drive high-performance and luxury cars, down here they have modest homes and cars that never turn a head. Whitehall drives a Renault Laguna.

WHITEHALL
The funny thing is that whenever I go out, like, people find out I'm a professional footballer and say 'Oh, you must be loaded', but it's not true at this level. You hear stories about certain clubs, like Preston, who are meant to be paying out a lot of money now, but they are isolated cases. Perhaps a chairman has come in with tons of money and started throwing it about, but that is not the norm. The norm is just ordinary wages. As I said, I took a drop in money to come here.

I don't think there's any sort of envy over top clubs' wages. It's just as it is, isn't it? No one thinks 'We should be getting more' or 'They should be getting less'. There's nothing we can do about it.

We'd all love to be up there and get that sort of money, but I think a lot of us know, especially those at 29, that our only chance is the lottery.

The fabled Scouse wit is expected, of course. He, in turn, is required to take the obligatory barbs. 'Oh yeah. You have to go along with everyone asking you for radios and wheel-trims and all stuff like that. But they're not very funny the rest of the lads, so someone's got to do it.'

That dart is aimed specifically at 'Trigger' Gray, who is apparently amusing himself by attempting to distract a singularly unimpressed Whitehall. Don't really see his getting that role in *Only Fools and Horses*. Stick to the keeping, Ian. Nicknames are compulsory in football teams. Whitehall is generally called Whitey but is also known as 'Roy', after Roy Gum, because his teeth tend not to be visible when he smiles, which he says is a legacy of a fall and the subsequent stitches in his top lip when he was a small boy. Deary has been 'Loafy' since his Blackpool days, when he had his hair shaved at the sides and what was left parted down the middle, like a loaf of bread.

Whitehall is unusual for a senior player in that he has no former League clubs.

WHITEHALL
I haven't an inkling into other clubs but I should imagine this is fairly typical of the sets of players. Probably all the other players, with the exception of one or two of the younger lads, have been at other professional clubs.

I've got to the end of next year on my contract here and at this stage I'd be very happy to sign another year. The sort of thing you have to think about is if you get your cards and can't find another club, how do you finance yourself for another year in college? That would be a bit of a struggle with two kids and the wife currently not working.

Ideally I'd like to get a job in football. I'll maybe do my coaching badge and look to get into coaching, management or physiotherapy, but it's being in the right place at the right time. If it doesn't work out for me in football then hopefully I'll be able to get some sort of job in a hospital or the community.

Right now my concern is Rochdale's slump. It's somewhat of a surprise in that we were going so well. It seems to have been a very sudden slump and quite strange, especially when you look at the goalscoring. At the end of October we were one of the top scoring teams in the country. All of a sudden, we don't score in six or seven games. When we were doing well we were getting a lot more balls in the box and there were more opportunities. The opportunities aren't there at the moment.

Goalscoring is a funny thing. It's hard to explain it. I don't feel there is added pressure on me. There'd be more pressure on me if everyone else was scoring and I was playing up front and *not* scoring. When the team is not scoring the pressure is on everyone. The team as a whole isn't playing well, we're not creating chances and we're not scoring goals.

Confidence is a great deal of it but not the entire reason. Confidence, again, is a funny thing. How much can you put down to confidence and how much to loss of concentration and all sorts of other things? The good thing about tonight is that we've put an end to the losing streak and it gives us some sort of basis to build on, a bit more confidence, a bit more self-belief. We've got Torquay at home on Saturday and if we get three points there we might be back to full confidence and get back on the road. We're only about six points off a play-off position, a couple of games, and there's still a lot of games between now and the end of the season, so we're definitely not out of it.

Docherty, returned from his audience with Kilpatrick, is studying a staff list and considering which players will be involved in the club's future. Of the 25 names, 10 will go at the end of the season.

DOCHERTY
One or two know already, but most don't, and I'll tell them when it suits the club. We may need them. The hard part is telling the YTS boys they won't be given jobs. A lot of them break down and cry. We try to do what we can to get them placed, write to other clubs, even non-League, to help them. Pros know the score so it's not as hard with them. These are things you have to do. I have my own position and the club as a whole to think about. It's my responsibility. Sometimes you have to make difficult decisions.

Docherty, too, has more immediate concerns. He is trying to revitalise the side but can forget about a chunk from the Liverpool match. Rochdale have now received their cut – £118,000 – but £75,000 will pay off the overdraft, £33,000 will go in tax and the rest will help cover wages.

DOCHERTY
I've had a good chat with the chairman, just review-ing the situation, and he's fine. We don't have a problem with each other. He's got the best interests of the club at heart, I know that. I've got to do what I can. These are the problems a manager has to deal with. It's the same for poor old Kevin Keegan at Newcastle, isn't it? He's struggling with Gillespie injured so he goes and spends £6.7m and £30,000 a week on Asprilla. Tough at the top, isn't it?

CHAPTER ELEVEN

Trial and Error

Rochdale's season goes into cold storage again, even if the League are reluctant to acknowledge the white stuff blanketing the country has the same effect at Spotland as elsewhere. The club makes the mistake of applying a little common sense and calling in a local referee the day before the scheduled match against Torquay to inspect the frozen, snow-bound pitch. His verdict is inevitable but the powers that be demand a further check by the match referee, on Saturday morning. The official, having travelled down from Hartlepool, now confirms the postponement and the players of Torquay, having turned up for the eight o'clock trip north, are sent home.

When you are constantly hearing 'It could only happen to Rochdale', you naturally assume paranoia has set in, but stick around long enough and you begin to wonder if they haven't got a point. Docherty is starting to suspect he is on the wrong end of a curse as his efforts to sign a striker continue to flounder. Inquiries about Trebble, the tormentor at Scarborough, and Burnley's John Francis have proved fruitless, and negotiations for Stockport's Ian Helliwell are in danger of going down the same plughole.

Money, of course, is the problem.

The Doc has had more luck in finding a replacement goalkeeper for Ian Gray, who suffered some reaction following the match at Scarborough. At the very least he needs a lengthy rest. He may even require another operation. Docherty has covered himself for a minimum of a month by taking on loan Kevin Pilkington, who recently deputised for Peter Schmeichel at Manchester United but, after the signing of Tony Coton, found himself number three in the Old Trafford pecking order.

'I'm delighted,' the manager says. 'Ian is still struggling so we had to do something. Kevin has a lot of potential and now he has a busy month to show what he can do.'

Chris Clarke, the goalkeeper overlooked by Dale, does not share Docherty's elation. 'I feel that Chris needs a breather to get his confidence back but no, he doesn't like it,' Docherty says. 'He's taken it badly, as you would expect. But I'm not here to make friends, I'm here to get results.'

Pilkington is soon acquainted with his new football environment, training beneath the stand because the freeze has eliminated their outdoor options and the cricket centre has a prior booking. Welcome to Rochdale.

The frost relents sufficiently to allow the match at Hartlepool – where Docherty launched his managerial career – to go ahead. The home side are reduced to ten men before half-time and Whitehall's 18th goal of the season puts Dale in front. Five minutes later, however, Pilkington pushes a free-kick against the frame of his goal and Hartlepool equalise from the rebound.

'Pilkington did all right,' Docherty says. 'He had no protection for the follow-up from the free-kick and we relaxed generally after we scored. Against ten men, we should have won.'

Winter tightens its icy grip again, forcing a second postponement of the home match against Preston, and by the end of the week Docherty is wishing it had not spared the Spotland meeting with Scarborough. Dale lose to two second-half goals and the groans reach Docherty from every direction. His team are down to 14th.

'The game is like that,' he says, resignedly. 'People can be fickle. I knew last October that it wouldn't be plain sailing. When people were saying we were certs for promotion and so on, I was warning that things could change. What's that about keeping your head when others are losing theirs? Fortunately, the dressing room is good, otherwise I might have jacked it in. Trouble is, I can't afford to jack it in.'

Being unable to afford the players he wants heightens his frustration. He hears on the radio that Helliwell has accepted a better offer from Burnley. He also has Williams back on his hands, the big striker returned from a loan spell with Chesterfield. Shaw's talks with Exeter have likewise come to nothing. The hapless Darren Ryan, on a week-to-week contract this season, is leaving. Docherty has been told to give him his cards.

'It's depressing,' the manager confesses. 'I can't get people in because of cost. Ryan's going, which saves £325 a week, but Williams is back, so that's another £500 a week back on the bill.'

His mood takes a turn for the better with the midweek home match against neighbours Bury. The atmosphere generated by a 3,000 crowd lifts Dale to their most convincing performance in weeks. Peake switches to left back while Thompstone manfully fills the troublesome striker's role and, if nothing else, makes a nuisance of himself. Butler shows his colleagues the way to goal, heading in after 63 minutes. A first League win since mid-November is taking shape until, 11 minutes from the end, Pilkington drops a cross and Bury equalise. Still, there is fun to be had from the self-deprecating, dark humour and the fans at the Sandy Lane end sing out 'Will we win in '96?' followed by 'We'll win again, don't know where, don't know when.'

On balance, Docherty concedes, he cannot complain. Bury were unfortunate not to have been awarded a goal early in the match, when Stuart appeared to head away from well behind the goal-line. 'He had rope marks on the back of his neck,' Docherty laughs. 'It was a much improved performance and Kevin's mistake was one of those things. He's very upset, but I've told him not to worry about it. Everyone makes mistakes and keepers are unlucky because they get punished more than outfield players. I've told him to forget it.'

That late blunder and a dank, drizzly morning have failed to dampen the enthusiasm of a father and son, collecting their tickets for Saturday's home match against Fulham. Les Duckworth, leaning on the reception hatch counter like an amiable corner shopkeeper, is content to serve up as much chat as the customers want. For a few moments a short, stout, elderly lady hovers patiently for attention but then feels entitled to interrupt.

'You men are all the same, talking about football. Just like my son,' she pecks.

The menfolk duly scatter and lay a red carpet of apologies. The woman brandishes a ticket for the Preston game, now scheduled for 12 March. 'My lad wants his money back. It's been called off twice and he can't come now because he's on nights.'

'When can he come?' Les asks, but the joke is lost on

the old dear. She stuffs the money in her purse without a change of expression.

'Best friend a man's got, his mother,' Les persists. She likes that. Yes, he'd make a good corner shopkeeper. Regular Arkwright, he is.

As she makes for the door she turns and asks: 'Who are they playing, anyway, on Saturday?'

'Fulham.'

'Should they win?'

'Oh, we'll win.'

Dealing with irate and abusive customers is not so easy.

'We got them on the phone after we lost at home last week. They're on saying "That's it, I'm never coming again". We even had one at half-time. He said: "I've come home. I can't stand any more of that and I shan't be coming again." But that's what you have to put up with. That's what it's like at Rochdale and we're used to it.'

The front doors are swinging open again as the players troop back from training. Apparently Docherty, rubbing his hands in self-congratulation, has been a bit of a star. One or two of his charges dispute that but they don't push their luck and, besides, they have more pressing business in the dressing room.

The players' judiciary system is about to wheel into action. In the dock is young Eddie, a YTS player, accused of not pulling his weight. This is regarded by the prosecution as a heinous offence and one which deserves no mercy. The court has boundless powers of punishment. At a recent trial the accused was sentenced to run a lap of the pitch – naked, and pursued by two colleagues wielding straps.

Young Eddie valiantly offers a defence, much to the

167

derision of the gallery. Acquittals are apparently uncommon and it does not look good for young Eddie. The court finds him guilty and the sentence is carried out. He is stripped and blacked head to toe in boot polish.

The roars of approval conjure images of Tyburn in the 18th century. What is it about cloistered, male communities that breeds this ritualistic pseudo-sadistic fetish? Clearly it is not a trait confined to public schools. High spirits spill into the corridor as players chase each other with cups of cold water. Is this really a team down and out after being deprived of a win for so long? You are reminded of Docherty's words: 'The dressing room is good.'

In a corner of the dressing room, a fair-haired player sits quietly, next to Gray, taking it all in. He is Kevin Pilkington, the 21-year-old goalkeeper signed on loan from Manchester United, but known in and around Rochdale this week as the culprit who threw away two points against Bury. The loan arrangement requires Dale to pay his wages of £550 a week, a modest figure by United's standards, but it makes him the best-paid player at Spotland. The incentive for Pilkington, however, is to give his career a kick-start.

PILKINGTON
United bought Tony Coton, and obviously he's got a lot more experience than me, but the gaffer said Rochdale wanted me on loan. I thought it would be a good chance to get a bit of experience, play a bit of League football and just generally hope to do well here. The move hasn't really affected my confidence. I'm only young, I've got a lot of time in front of me.

We all make mistakes and I learned a lot from our

Coca-Cola Cup game against York, when we lost 3–0. It's all a learning process. I don't really know anything about football at this level, but David Beckham went to Preston last season and enjoyed it, and this year he's been playing in the first team at United. Ben Thornley and Terry Cooke have been out on loan to lower division clubs this season, as well.

They obviously don't play as much football at this level as United do but they try, they really try, and that's good. The actual clubs and facilities are very different. Last week here we were struggling for somewhere to train. We went up to the indoor cricket club and one day we had a five-a-side in the snow, across at the park there, which was good fun. At United, the first team will go to Old Trafford, where they've got the undersoil heating on, or they go into the big gym.

The lads here ask me a lot of questions about what it's like there and I tell them the first-team players always make you feel welcome. It's good. They want to know here what Eric Cantona is really like, that sort of thing, and I don't really mind.

He's a legend. You see some of the stuff he does in training and it's unbelievable; his finishing and his tricks. Giggsy, as well. He's top class. Eric is a bit quiet in the dressing room, but then I'm not really in the first-team dressing room, I'm still with the young lads. But he talks to you and he'll sign autographs all day for the fans. He's really good that way. Also I'm being asked for tickets here. With the United–City FA Cup tie coming up on Sunday, I'm a popular man. I don't mind. I've sorted some out for them and I'll be there, definitely. The lads here have been great. They've made me very welcome.

No wonder. But then Pilkington comes over as shy and unassuming – hardly a clone of Peter Schmeichel – and still enjoys returning to his roots and his chums at home in Derbyshire.

PILKINGTON

Whenever I'm at home I go and watch the lads play in the local team and it's the same sort of atmosphere, really. They all enjoy their football and like a good laugh, and if the lads back home ever think I'm getting too big for my boots they'll bring me down. I imagine it would be the same here.

[Tuesday's costly error effectively ruled out any likelihood of arrogance anyway.] As a goalkeeper you can't hide. Like me on Tuesday night. I dropped it and their lad's there just to knock it in. I was upset over that. I was in two minds. When I first came for it I thought I'd punch it, then I thought no, I'd got time to catch it. In the end it was just a stupid mistake. It makes it even worse when you are trying to help a team out.

Doc was very good about it. He had a word with me afterwards and said we all make these mistakes, I've just got to learn from it. When I went to United they told me goalkeepers don't peak until 25 or 26, sometimes later. Look at the keepers around now who are over 30.

I don't know if the loan here will be extended beyond the month. It depends on Ian Gray's fitness. I don't mind as long as I'm playing, getting the experience and enjoying it. Perhaps I'll go out on loan to a few more clubs, but I've certainly not given up on United. The gaffer hasn't said a lot to me but you've just got to keep trying and hopefully knock on the door some time. Hopefully I can develop over that period and then get another contract. My fiancée and I are planning to get married at the end of next season.

Pilkington is given sympathetic treatment by Whitehall who, after beating him for the umpteenth time during the kick-in, before the home match against Fulham, retrieves the ball from the net and gently heads it into the keeper's arms. Every clean catch by Pilkington is greeted with ironic cheers, although any goodwill in the air over Spotland evaporates as Rochdale toil. Stuart gives the home team an early lead but Fulham equalise and in the second half Jimmy Hill's club, despite being reduced to 10 men, resist Dale's laboured endeavours to regain the advantage.

Moulden and Taylor are sent on in the hope of finding a spark, but to no avail. That old favourite of the football charts, 'What a load of rubbish', serenades Docherty's men. Fulham, second from bottom, secure a precious point and their chairman thrusts out that famous chin as he vigorously applauds his players off the field. Dale, now 15th, creep away in embarrassment, boos and jeers hounding them up the tunnel.

'You can't blame the supporters,' Docherty says. 'It's understandable. We've played badly and they're entitled to give us stick. It happens. You don't like it but you'd better get used to it if you want to be involved in this game. Overall, I've got to say, the fans have been patient.'

The manager's patience in negotiations is rewarded with another loan agreement, this time to bring a former employee, veteran striker Dave Lancaster, from Bury for a month. Priced out of every other avenue, Docherty is content 'The Bomber' will enhance the potency of his attack.

'I've tried loads of players at loads of clubs but we just can't manage the sort of money I'm being asked for. I'm sure Lanky will do a good job for us. Okay, so he's no spring chicken, but he's a good pro, knows the game and leads the line well.'

Outside, Big Willo is loading his stuff into the back of a trendy four-wheel-drive vehicle. If it's not this, it's a sporty little number, or a BMW. His trappings are not those of a typical Third Division player, but then he is married to the daughter of Stockport County's wealthy chairman, has interests in property and patently is not dependent on his £500 a week from Rochdale. He does, though, appear to need the football.

'It was a pity we couldn't get it sorted out at Chester-field because they are going well in the Second Division and it would have been much nearer my home,' he says. 'I did all right in the games I played, scored goals and I was hopeful, but there was a problem with the money, I think. The boss promised me a run in the first team here but I got another injury, and I'm just getting back to fitness again.'

In Williams's absence, Lancaster makes his debut at Northampton and optimism gradually percolates through Rochdale's play again. The portents prove reliable and Thompstone, relieved of frontline duties at the start, arrives as a substitute to score, 10 minutes from the end. To their cost, they think it's all over. Northampton come back from the dead, score twice, and Dale are defeated again.

'Unprofessional,' Docherty growls. 'Totally unprofessional. We've played well, got the lead and done the hard part. But we thought we'd won it and that's where we got it wrong. We hadn't won it. We had to keep our discipline and see the game out. So instead of three points we've got none. We've thrown the game away.'

He clings to some consolation in Lancaster's contribution. 'He did his stuff and I've got to be pleased with him. He gave us what we'd been missing – a big, powerful presence up front but also the ability to read the game and give us the leadership we've been looking for.'

Back home the fans are not so readily appeased. The local paper carries a postbag of heartfelt pleas. The chairman and his colleagues on the board take the brunt of the criticism. They are called upon to act – and soon. And another thing, what happened to the Liverpool money?

There is a sense of relief inside the club that the next fixture is away, at Mansfield. It happens. Home advantage can be a contradiction in terms. When the household is full of squabbles rather than comfort, the road is far more enticing.

Dale – and the diehards – make it to the East Midlands to be told the match is doubtful because of heavy rain. Docherty and his counterpart, Andy King, tiptoe across the sodden pitch, each with his own opinion: Docherty is keen to play and King, with a depleted side, is not so keen.

'I can understand that,' Docherty says. 'Eight players out, I'd be the same. But I think we should give it a go.'

The referee, not fully recovered from being scolded by the groundsman for walking on the pitch, is wary of 'giving it a go' only to be put in the invidious position of having to abandon the match. Instead, with 40 minutes to kick-off and the rain ceased, he postpones it and Rochdale have another entry in their catalogue of calamities.

According to the pools panel, no one missed much, anyway. They deem it a no-score draw. 'Even they've got us sussed,' Jimmy Robson says drily.

The next game is at home. The visitors are Lincoln City, a struggling team, and one they should beat, but it sounds an all-too-familiar trap. Jason Peake splashes through black puddles the size of duck ponds in the car park behind the condemned enclosure and painstakingly treads a meandering route to the main entrance.

'We desperately need to win this,' he says, veering away from another watery hazard. 'Got to. They're putting the knife in at the fanzine, the supporters are having a go. We're having a rough time. But we can get it together again. I know we can. I hate playing against Lincoln, though. Their manager, the way he plays, it's all long balls.'

In the Rochdale manager's office, Docherty shows no obvious sign of wounding. He is relaxed and smiling, even if he still has no money to spend. 'I said to the chairman that if we'd not had that Liverpool money we would still have an overdraft, so why not have one now? But he wouldn't budge.'

Docherty takes one of his constitutional walks and returns with the look of a man who's found a knife in his back.

'I've just bawled out four of them for drinking,' he barks. 'They said it was only shandy. I said I don't care, dump it. I've gone berserk with them, in public.

The way we're going, that's all we need the punters to see.'

'Who were they?' Robson asks.

'Butler, Taylor, Hall, Hardy. Bloody players. They don't think. Drives you mad.'

'It's got you going, anyway.'

'Too true it has. That's definitely got me at it now. Done me a favour.'

Robson takes over bawling duties when a YTS player pops his head through the door. The unsuspecting youngster is told to get his colleagues together and write a letter of apology for leaving college early the other day. He protests his innocence but Robson's judgement is that they are all culpable. 'Get it done.'

As the door closes Robson shakes his head. 'They've been shooting off an hour early. They've got to do their college bit but they don't see it. They don't like it, they get bored, or whatever. But it's like a lot of things, it comes down to attitude. You look for lads who've got that, as well as ability.'

Lancaster's attitude is one of his attractions for Docherty and the massive centre-forward is given an appropriately expansive welcome back to Spotland by the public address announcer, who presumably was selected for his wonderfully unfettered local accent. The Bomber duly landed, Dale have to contend with the predicted aerial bombardment from John Beck's team, and Butler's absence is proving a distinct handicap.

So is Pilkington's continued uncertainty in goal and Kilpatrick, sitting in isolation at the far top corner of the directors' box, is anxiously drawing on his cigarette. It is not difficult to find room tonight. 'It's a very small crowd,' the voice of hospital radio tells his listeners. 'I've seen bigger for reserve games.'

He should be thankful he has plenty of incident to describe. In the 19th minute, Valentine is left stranded and Pilkington is beaten at the second attempt. The groans gain volume with every misplaced pass and Peake, again deployed at left-back, receives a volley of abuse for losing the sense of direction earlier displayed around the black puddles.

Dale's hopes are buoyed when Lincoln's keeper is penalised in the area for a foul on Whitehall. The keeper is livid and has a case. Alas, he also has a booking and Dale have a penalty. Whitehall converts it, left-footed, into the bottom right-hand corner, as consummately as you will ever see a penalty converted. It is his 19th goal of the season and the home team are back in business.

The pitch, covered during the day, is playing reasonably well and accommodates Dale's surge of confidence. The state of the surface would appear irrelevant to Lincoln although they are, ironically, caught out deep into stoppage time at the end of the first half by Lancaster's flicked header, from which Stuart puts Rochdale ahead. The man voicing The Imps' match report service is beside himself with outrage. Where did the referee get the extra time from? Where did Rochdale get their goal from? He depicts a travesty of justice. However Beck sees it, he spends most of the break in the dugout with only his fags for company.

The broad smiles in the home directors' box would indicate no one there is disturbed by events. The Doc has a sprightly step as he heads for the dressing room and Dale's supporters are slightly numbed. They have no cause to jeer yet and are ill-prepared to cheer. The lady who works behind the boardroom bar senses the importance as acutely as Peake had. 'They'll be shouting for Doc's head if they lose this,' she says.

Docherty plans to avert such an eventuality by shuffling his pack and switching Peake to his accustomed role in midfield. Within two minutes of the re-start, however, Lincoln are level. Ten minutes on and Dale lead again, Stuart's splendidly driven shot burying itself into the far bottom corner. Kilpatrick is sitting back, drawing on his cigarette contentedly.

The anxiety regenerates every time Lincoln toss the ball into Pilkington's goal mouth. His nervous handling sustains the visitors' optimism, although he is nowhere near laying a glove on the fateful pass played in after 73 minutes. Stuart, under no pressure from an opponent, intervenes and inexplicably turns the ball into his own goal. Whitehall goes close deep into yet more stoppage time but the man with The Imps update is spared a coronary.

The Rochdale Press contingent make their way through the bar, down the stairs and into Docherty's office for his verdict.

'They are horrible, aren't they?' he opens. 'I'd rather pack up than play like that. They are a disgrace. It's just long ball, playing for corners and throw-ins. No wonder their number 10 went off – his arms must have been aching after taking all those long throws. I told the players at half-time "For the sake of football, you've got to beat this lot." I don't talk to Beck. I don't like him, so why should I? I don't see the point.'

The local Press boys are to the point, deriding Pilkington as a joke and suggesting Docherty might have been better served playing Big Willo in goal. Where was Pilkington for the third goal? And what was Stuart doing? And by the way, does that count as a hat trick and mean he gets the match ball?

The scribes' elder, who is due to retire in a couple of months, asks the Doc if he is likely to see another win before he goes. 'If we don't, I could be out of a job,' Docherty retorts.

There are no signs here of the fawning or sycophancy some of the more illustrious figures in the game expect and experience with the national media. Docherty enjoys the crack and appreciates the candid relationship.

Next call on his post-match round of duties is the boardroom. Beck is chatting near the bar but the two managers never face each other. Docherty speaks to Rod Brierley, who has a leg in plaster after a mishap, and some of the ladies gathered round a table. Then he makes his way to Kilpatrick and Morris.

The message is consistent: 'I keep reaching into my drawer for a stick-on smile but I'm running out of them . . . They drive you mad . . . I changed it at half-time because Bayliss wasn't doing it, same with Martin, and I thought Peakey might unlock them.'

Beck heads for the door, spreading a general 'Goodnight', but Docherty ignores him. Kilpatrick catches his manager's attention with some swingeing remarks about 'that goalkeeper we've been lumbered with'.

Morris adds his two penn'orth: 'I'm terrified every time the ball is crossed.'

Docherty throws up his hands, offering no defence – it must be contagious. 'Blame me for Pilkington,' he says. 'Blame me. Lack of communication is a big problem. He's not a talker.'

But it is not all down to the keeper, as Kilpatrick goes

on to confess. 'What I can't understand is why we're so different from earlier in the season, when even if the other side got two or three we would still win. Now when we get in their half we don't seem to know what to do.'

'Losing Gray and Butler have been big blows,' confesses Docherty, 'and now Thompstone has got to have X-rays on a suspected fracture at the bridge of his nose. He was unconscious after that collision with the keeper.'

They return, inexorably, to the subject of money. Tonight's attendance has not helped Docherty's cause. At 1,253, it is the smallest crowd for a League match this season.

Kilpatrick tells him: 'You could have £200,000, no problem, if we sold, for example, Butler for £500,000.'

Docherty leaves with that tantalising thought and Kilpatrick gives him what sounds ominously like the one thing no manager seeks – a vote of confidence.

'There's no way Mick Docherty's job is in jeopardy. It's his first year as the manager and he's done, on the whole, a good job. He's made perhaps one and a half mistakes as far as players are concerned – Shaw and Hardy. Of course we're disappointed the way things have gone in recent weeks, just as our supporters are. But in the end we have to face facts – financial facts.'

Kilpatrick confirms Docherty will have to trim his squad to about 16 players next season. 'We just can't afford to carry more than that.'

Docherty mulls over his goalkeeping dilemma for the next 48 hours. Does he persist with Pilkington? Does he give Clarke another chance? Neither of those options inspires him with confidence. And he has to forget about Gray for the rest of the season, because he is to have another hernia operation. Docherty scours the staff lists of other clubs and comes back to a name he has been attracted to before: Lance Key, Sheffield Wednesday's third-choice keeper, who is available on loan. The deal is done.

'Pilkington was disappointed because we could have kept him on for another game, but I decided I couldn't do that,' Docherty says. 'It didn't work out for him or for us and you have to accept these things. The game can be hard. I just hope for his sake he gets it together. But we can't wait for that to happen. We have to get on with our lives. That's the way it is.'

CHAPTER TWELVE

Beyond a Joke

Any laughs have been strained this week, but unfettered mirth returns from an unlikely source. There again, Rochdale watchers, familiar with the perverse nature of their team, will tell you it is no surprise to them that a first win in almost three months should be achieved away to Preston North End, the high-fliers with the facilities and resources to match their ambition. First-half goals by Whitehall and Stuart, and stubborn resistance from Key and Butler, clamp the points.

A beaming Docherty is fulsome in his praise of the new goalkeeper and his trusty central defender: 'Key made a big difference, he's got good hands, gave the lads confidence . . . Butler's got this foot injury but he battles on superbly . . .'

He is also comforted by a whisper from Dawson, that three players told him they were 'pleased for the boss'.

'To a certain extent,' Docherty says, 'criticism washes over me, just as I don't get carried away with praise. You know the people can be cheering you one match and calling for your head the next. But it is nice when you hear something like that from the players. I like to think they appreciate the way I treat them. We've all been lifted by this result. The play-offs are still possible. We're 10 points off a play-off place, with 14 games to go. We've got five out of six at home, big games. Anything can happen.'

Butler rests his sore foot on the Monday after the win at Deepdale but has important business at the secretary's office, checking how many bookings he and some of his colleagues are from suspension. Les Duckworth, armed with a one-liner for every occasion, teases: 'He's got more bookings than Bernard Manning.'

Docherty is hoping to book Valentine as his coach next season and already the 32-year-old central defender is sharing the load at training sessions. 'Peter's legs have gone but he still has a lot to offer this club and he is respected by the players. He got his coaching badge last summer and I'd like him to coach here. We'd keep his registration so he could play if necessary for the first team, and also for the reserves to help bring them along.'

The manager and players report for more poignant duty the following morning. Docherty had received a letter from a man whose 17-year-old daughter had been taken ill and died. The girl, a Rochdale fan, was to be laid to rest in her old Dale shirt. The club arranged for a new, signed shirt to be sent to the father and, unannounced, Docherty and the players joined the mourners at the girl's funeral.

Later in the week, Docherty receives another letter from the father, expressing his appreciation. 'I wasn't a Dale fan before,' he wrote, 'but I am now.'

Docherty has had to draw heavily on his compassion of late. Young Taylor lost his grandfather and needed a sensitive boss to lean on. Now Butler has learned his mother is gravely ill and Docherty tells him he can miss Saturday's home match against Leyton Orient if he feels too distressed to play, but Butler tells Docherty that his mum wants him to play, so he'll play for her. Counselling is all in a day's work for a football manager.

DOCHERTY
You can go from one extreme to another. You can have players squaring up to each other, and we've had it here. Deary's done it and Willo had a bust-up with Thackeray recently. Generally I let them sort it out, I think it's the best way. As long as they do, and shake hands at the end, that's fine. We used to have a bust-up a week at Burnley.

But no matter how hard or macho they want to be, they all have their feelings and there are times when they need that little bit of thought from the manager. It's not just the players, it's other members of staff and their families. My dad taught me the importance of the little things – a bunch of flowers here and there, just to show you care.

Docherty's agenda also includes mapping out his scouting missions over the next week or so, the grind of watching future opponents and players who just might come within Dale's financial range.

DOCHERTY
I try to take in at least one game a week and up to three. These days, they tend to be fairly local. I used to travel the length and breadth of the country, until the chairman saw my expenses and clipped

my wings. That's the difference between me and
Alex Ferguson. He can fly to Milan to see a player
if he wishes, no questions asked. Having said that,
I don't know if I would like to be a top manager,
with however many thousands of pounds a week
they earn. You're always in the public eye, you've
always got the media and cameras to face. I enjoy
some privacy. It's important to me.

Docherty is at ease with the usual Press men after another
win, 1–0 against Orient. Crap match but we got three
points. Key did well again, and Lanky deserved the goal
for the way he's been playing.'

Lanky also deserved a long-awaited tribute from David
Ainley, the tannoy voice of Spotland. Ainley taped the
theme music from *Dambusters* ready to celebrate the
next goal The Bomber might score during his previous
spell here, two seasons ago. But he failed to score again
before his departure. Now the long-overdue opportunity
has arrived, only for Ainley to realise he left the tape at
home. Next time Bomber, next time . . .

The twice postponed home game against Preston is
about to go ahead despite attempts by the elements
to intervene again. A brutally cold night and a pitch
three-parts covered by snow perfectly complement the
sprigs of holly and Yuletide greetings on the front of the
programme. So they weren't dumped, after all. At least
there's a loose sheet inside bringing punters up to date.
Well, not quite. It says 12 February. For the record, this
is 12 March.

Little wonder Rochdale play as though they don't know
what day it is. Perhaps the orange ball has something to

do with it. There is always something slightly surreal and festive about a white pitch and a coloured ball, and Dale are as generous as a disorientated Santa. Stuart is relieved of the ball by Paul Birch, on loan from Wolves and a cut above most at this level. He plants the ball in the top corner of Key's goal, and Deary's awful back-pass presents Preston with a second before half-time.

Docherty takes off Martin and Whitehall, who was a doubtful starter because of an attack of gastroenteritis, and sends on Williams and Thompstone. Someone down at the front of the main stand is patently unaware of Whitehall's debility and whips himself into a frenzy of incredulity and consternation, his head on a swivel, seeking out concurrence, explanation, or something . . . 'Top scorer! He's taken off the top scorer!'

With the switch in personnel comes a change in tactics. Now Doc is unashamedly aiming for the twin towers of Lancaster and Williams, and Preston are finding them a handful. Chances are squandered and valid appeals for a penalty, as Deary tumbles, are rejected. There is no way back. You know it. They know it. Sure enough, Preston snap out of it and snaffle a third. Birch is allowed to work space on the right and his centre is knocked past a stationary Key.

The avalanche of derision, briefly contained by that semblance of a recovery, descends on Docherty and his players again. 'Get that stump off,' is the plaintive cry from the heart of the stand.

Those in wheelchairs, parked at the front, are among the more forthright.

'This is a joke, Docherty.'

'Useless git, Williams.'

'That's it, Thackeray, give it to a red shirt.'

'Gerrit sorted, Docherty.'

'Get Russell on, Docherty.'

Eleven minutes from the end, Docherty does get Russell on, but it is no more than a gesture. The game is up. Hordes make for the exit accompanied by the chanting of the Preston fans: 'Bye-bye, bye-bye. Bye-bye, bye-bye.'

The bravehearts who stick it out to the bitter end are taunted with 'Going up, going up, going up,' but have the spirit and wit to retort, 'Staying down, staying down, staying down'. This is a time for gallows humour.

Tonight's attendance is disclosed as 4,597. 'There won't be 500 for the next match,' a voice from a wheelchair prophesies. More than half this crowd are Preston supporters, who find more amusement in the rapidly emptying terraces. 'It's like Chorley,' one scorns. 'Chorley's not as bad as this,' another says, prolonging the laughter.

Cruel joke it may be, but they have a point. Spotland has taken on a desolate, forlorn countenance. It's as if the ghost of displaced Christmas past is delivering its chilling message: 'Forget those fantasies about promotion'. More squabbles behind the scenes with the Council and the rugby club threaten to hold up the building of the new stand, yet will it be necessary, anyway, the cynics are asking.

Bury, not unreasonably, bar Lancaster from playing against them but Rochdale still manage a creditable draw, Butler's early goal and much subsequent sweat serving to eke a point. Docherty rewards his players by sending them bowling instead of training the following Monday, even though they have a match on the Tuesday evening. 'Suppose they'll be golfing tomorrow,' someone sarcastically muses.

Docherty is unrepentant: 'You can over-train players at this time of the year and do more harm than good.'

Not that the manager is involved in trying for strikes. He is more interested in a striker, Lancaster. He agrees a deal with Bury to keep the player, on loan, for the rest of the season and has an option for his services, which he plans to exercise, next season. Docherty will discuss his retained list with directors before the home match against Torquay and tell the YTS players their fate afterwards. Financial restraints mean that only two of the six second-year youngsters will be offered jobs. A third, sidelined by injury, will have another chance. To Docherty's dismay, he is told he cannot afford to keep on Valentine as coach, unless he trades a player.

The football is a relief. Dale win 3–0, Whitehall claiming the second from the penalty spot, his ninth conversion from nine this season. With three victories and a draw from five games and another home fixture coming up, the sniff of a play-off place still lingers. Who's for golf?

Training is back on the menu come Friday morning, but beef is not. The latest chapter in the mad cow disease saga has sent a scare coursing through the nation and Les Duckworth has responded. 'We've changed the meal tomorrow to chicken,' he explains. 'It's usually beef, and it's very good, but you don't want sponsors turning up and saying 'I'm not having this'. So it's chicken in a white wine sauce. Lovely. You have to think of everything.'

Someone from the Stadium Company pops his head through the hatch and passes on the message that Wigan are bringing 1,000 fans to the match, almost as many as Dale drew the other night. The attendance of 1,206 again lowered the season's record. 'We need all we can get,' Duckworth says. 'We've tried everything to encourage them – now it's kids free, £1 off for adults. We've done all sorts over the years.'

Just as those endeavours cannot make Rochdale AFC compulsive viewing, so they have no bearing on some of the club's wider appeal. In, for instance, Norway. And Australia.

It can only be assumed those long, dark Scandinavian winters have a strange effect on the natives. One of their number, postman Jarle Gunstad, learned of this 'little club' in the North-West of England and thought why not take a look at them rather than Manchester United or Liverpool? Very long, very dark winters. That first visit failed to cure Jarle, and now his branch of the Supporters' Club boasts 50 members. He organises occasional trips to Spotland and keeps his barmy army in touch with Dale developments through the pages of his regular news bulletin.

The Australian connection also arrived out of curiosity. An ex-pat made good Down Under, retracing his roots, was unaccountably lured to Spotland, politely requesting if he might take a look. Of course he could, and now his regular trips to the Old Country routinely include visits to the home of Rochdale AFC. Other wealthy, long-distance fans include a racehorse owner based in Guernsey. Their patronage has run to a few donations, but as yet a Jack Walker has not materialised. Duckworth can only hope, and does not push.

'They've got cash, they know we haven't, and if they want to come in and help us in a big way they will,' Duckworth says. 'They can see the situation without my telling them. You can frighten people away.'

Duckworth was eased into the Spotland fold, a process which began 15 years ago. A Mancunian and, worse still in the minds of the paranoid in these parts, a Manchester United fan, he moved to Rochdale to run a pub. 'I'd never been this side of Manchester. It was like coming into another world.'

Even so, he soon found his way around the local social and sporting scene. The son of a comedian, he had the patter and personality to make an impression and the show business nous to make good use of his football contacts. He supplied the club with drinks, set up a bar and, in his words, 'dragged people to the executive club'. He can laugh now: 'When it rained, there was an inch of water on the floor.'

He had a spell with Middleton Cricket Club before joining Rochdale AFC full-time. As marketing manager he is responsible for sponsorship and promotional matters, such as making deals for perimeter advertising and the space on the front of the shirt. He is mildly chuffed to have negotiated an extension of a contract with Carcraft for that slot on the players' chests and the distinction of being official club sponsor.

DUCKWORTH
If there's any hint of money parting company with its owner, I'm there. I'm the wheeler-dealer; I have to be. There's no doubt that results on the field determine the success on the marketing side. That's why a poor finish to the season, which we've tended to have, hits us quite badly. It's that much harder to attract money for the following season. It can be a thankless task. Mention Rochdale to some and they turn their noses up and laugh.

189

The showman and businessman in Duckworth also knows how to milk an audience and turn Rochdale's humble status to their advantage. Small, middle-aged, with a comic's active face, he is a natural compere at the theatre of no dreams.

DUCKWORTH
A lot come from bigger clubs and of course it's very different here. It can be embarrassing for sponsors when we've brought guests who aren't familiar with football at this level, so I humour them, have a bit of fun with them. You can't ignore the fact that it's only Rochdale – but you can use it. Say we have a competition, guess the time of the first goal. I'll tell them, 'Try Monday'. Or I'll say, 'Got nothing better to do on a Saturday?' I'll go up to the ladies and say, 'There's a television over here. It's a nice Bette Davis film on BBC 2 at three o'clock. Forget this rubbish.' Nine times out of ten they say they've enjoyed it and want to come again.

Docherty punches the security combination to let himself into the office. He needs a copy of a letter he is sending to his old sparring partner, John Beck. So they do communicate, after all!

'Not really,' Docherty mutters and grudgingly signs the letter. 'He wrote complaining about what I'd said after their match here. He said I was unprofessional. Anyway, the chairman wants me to smooth things over.'

To that end, Docherty claims in his reply that his comments were taken out of context by the Press, that he merely said he wouldn't play the same style football as Beck. It is not an original ploy among football folk.

Feed the Press a story, then blame them if you get any flak. It's all part of what makes the game go round.

So is a regular supply of team news and club information through the local media outlets. Still clutching his letter to Beck, Docherty takes a call from Mike Brookes at Duckworth's desk and runs through his planned line-up for tomorrow's match. Approaching 10 o'clock, the fuzzed images of the players begin to pass by the hatch's sliding window, making for the dressing room to change for training.

In an adjoining office, Karen Smyth is 'having a bad morning'. Graham Morris has informed her the admission price to the away fans' enclosure tomorrow is to be put up. Under the regulations they are entitled to make such an increase provided the customers in that section enjoy a particular privilege. The enclosure is covered and that, Rochdale are satisfied, complies with the requirement. It also means some frantic admin work for Karen.

So what is a nice girl like her doing in a place like this? Karen, 24, single, blonde, is a Yorkshire lass and came to Spotland after being made redundant at Halifax Town, four years ago. She worked in the commercial department as assistant to Steve Walmsley before succeeding Keith Clegg as club secretary.

SMYTH
Football is not a bad environment for a woman. More and more women are coming into the game now. It is perhaps as well that I am unattached because the hours are long, you are here on match days and match nights, and you've got to show your face at functions, as well. But it is also a lot of fun. No two days are the same and I don't

191

think you can get an atmosphere quite like it in any other job.

People are intrigued when they find out where I work. They think football is just players and nothing else. It's definitely busier when we are doing well – such as in the build-up to the Liverpool Cup tie. But it's also very busy in the close season, when we're making arrangements for the following season and having to cover for colleagues on holiday. On a day such as this, with a match tomorrow, we have to go round the ground checking the terracing, the turnstiles, the lighting, the toilets, the blowers and so on.

Another, unspecified part of the job, you suspect, is playing nurse-maid to spoiled footballers – and coping with the dressing-room vernacular.

SMYTH
My door into the corridor is opposite the door to the dressing room so I hear the language and you learn to close your ears to it. You also know you are going to be in for some leg-pulling, but you get used to it and give them as much as they give you. If you are going to get their confidence, which I think is important, you've got to do that and be on a par with them. Players are always knocking on the door; Can I do this, can I do that? I do sometimes think I shouldn't be doing some of the things they ask but I do so to keep the peace. [Keeping the peace with irate fans is a task that requires patience and diplomacy.] Somebody came in and had a good moan after we won 3–0. Said it was about time we won. The one

thing I *hate* is when we come round to the time for the retained list – and it's coming up now. Players know what it's about and that it will happen to some of them, but when it does and their jobs are taken away it seems very hard. Especially when the players in question have families. You get to know them and like them – and suddenly they're out of work. Every year the list of available players circulated by the League and PFA gets longer.

Unless Rochdale's gates improve dramatically, they will continue to add names to those lists. 'From the 1,200 crowd we had the other night we are actually left with about £800,' Karen says. 'All right, so we've taken season tickets and box money in advance, but receipts like that don't even scratch the surface of what is required.'

She admits her knowledge of the game is limited ('I'd never been to a football ground until I started at Halifax, though I understand a lot more than I did'), but there is no shortage of comment – informed or otherwise – behind that hatch window. Tom Nichol, who works part-time, mainly making arrangements and organising officials for reserve and junior games, has a wealth of experience and contacts.

DUCKWORTH
He's done everything in the game and still keeps in touch with the schoolboy scene for any tip-off about promising players. Mind you, even *he* doesn't get any favours here. He had a testimonial after 40 years – 40 years! – and got charged on the

car park to come to his own match. Could only happen here.

Tom appears just after 11 o'clock and the rest – Keith Clegg and his wife still muck in – eagerly anticipate the mid-morning treat. 'Tom's in charge of the biscuits,' Les explains in an exaggerated tone. Tom takes the hint.

NICHOL
This club has always been known for looking after visitors. Scouts from other clubs always loved coming here for the spread, you know. I'm sure it was the food rather than the players. The pies were the thing. Everywhere in the game people talked about our pies. Jim Finney, the referee, used to ask us to bring some down whenever we were in his area.

Rochdale may have moved on to chicken in a white wine sauce, but it remains, in idiomatic terms, a pie and peas club. On the desk in the centre of the main office sits a bulky typewriter rather than a state-of-the-art computer. Or even an antiquated computer. Tossed to one side is a glossy brochure from Silverstone and a covering letter, extolling the wonders of their fast-lane corporate hospitality service. Les laughs: 'I don't think we're quite in that league.'

Next door you'll find, as apparently most people do, much to Steve Walmsley's irritation, the club shop. To the right of the displayed shirts, scarves, programmes and sundry other souvenirs is a cubbyhole otherwise known as Walmsley's office. And the office of David Lord, his assistant. This is another source of irritation for Walmsley. A portly, balding figure, though not yet 42, he has a reputation for being truculent, recalcitrant – and exceedingly good at his job.

Walmsley's job, as commercial manager, is not only to run the shop and put together the programme, but to mastermind the organisation of the lottery and draw funds which are vital to the survival of Rochdale AFC. He hails from Bolton and was raised on a balanced diet of football, watching Bolton Wanderers, and rugby league, at Wigan and Swinton. The grains of a selling career grew with a bread round, in Blackburn, but the allure of football, and the Wanderers in particular, brought him back to Burnden Park, where he built up the weekly draw and exploited the potential of the then new scratch-off lottery tickets. Via Rochdale Hornets, Swinton and Blackpool FC, he arrived at Spotland at the beginning of 1991.

WALMSLEY
They'd had about 10 commercial managers in as many years and I'd been here only two weeks when the manager, Terry Dolan, left for Hull City. So I was at a club that had no home game for about seven weeks because of the weather, the manager had gone, no weekly draw, no lottery and no proper club shop. I started from absolutely nothing. In two years we had one of the biggest weekly draws in the bottom two divisions.

With all the problems of the National Lottery, three-quarters of all the clubs have packed in the weekly draws and lotteries in the past 12 months. We still have one of the biggest in the country. It has always produced the goods, regardless of what has been done on the field, or the gates we've got.

It's all about population, if you can get it right. I would never succeed at Scarborough. Only 42,000 live there. If you turn right, you've nothing but fish; if you turn left, you've nothing but sheep.

I'm good at what I do and I like what I do. I taught myself from being a salesman at Warburton's Bread. The main thing is the organising of door-to-door collecting, building up the membership through newsagents, door-to-door canvassing and so on. We've been badly hit by the National Lottery, but we've joined up with Premier Instant, a £1 scratch-off, and that's pulled back a lot. Last year we made a profit of £169,000. This year I would say it will still be more than £100,000. And this club has been losing perhaps £5,000 to £6,000 a week. With wages and all the other costs it takes probably £16,000 to £17,000 a week to run this club, which is no more than some of the top Premier League players earn. But on gates of 2,000 or less . . . I told the directors that at their Lincoln match they took £3,800 when my office took £11,500 that week. They finally accepted it's nothing to do with football.

The directors here have kept this club going for years and years, but there are things they admit they've done wrong. In football, though, people never learn from their mistakes. It's like no other business. All the time there are fans on the terraces who think they could do the manager's job, the secretary's job, or my job, but if they spent six months working inside a club they'd run away screaming. I have never known a small body of people, like at this club, work so hard, for so long, for so much to go wrong.

As with all clubs, the busiest office is the commercial office, but it is also the smallest room in the building. I live, breathe and sleep what I do. I regularly work more than 60 hours a week. The pressure recently has made me ill again and I ended up seeing a specialist. I have had problems at football and rugby league clubs for 21 years. None of them are any different. When Len Shackleton left that blank page in his book, under the heading 'What Directors Know About Football', he should have made it a full bloody blank book. Directors are the bane of my life.

There again, directors have not always been best pleased with him. He was given a yellow card over that rumpus with Clubcall, and a red after a fracas with an executive box spectator, although evidently that has not taken effect. The point is, he does seem to generate friction. There was also that business with the PR man.

WALMSLEY
People try things on with little clubs like this that they'd never try with Liverpool, Everton, United and City. What was happening with Clubcall was an insult to our intelligence. The last bill was £1,020, out of which we got £60 or £70. So we decided to do our own, with Telephone Information Service. Mike Brookes does it on a voluntary basis and we get 50 per cent. We told Clubcall we weren't renewing the contract and to take the line out. They didn't, it was used and they sent us the bill. I didn't pay it and when they contacted us I told them what I thought of them and put the phone down. They wrote a great

long letter to the chairman, said they would take us to court and in the end we paid the bill.

The lad brought in as a PRO was greener than green. He was being paid for doing what Les Duckworth and I do for nothing. He was a joke. I actually wrote two pages of the daft things he'd done to give to the chairman, but before I did he had disappeared. Any chance the fanzine get to have a go at me, they take. They will always try to put us down. Francis Collins worked for me for two years and I've never known anybody work so hard. He was brilliant. But he has a mind of his own like no one I've ever come across. Players at this club have said, 'If I get hold of him I'll rip him apart.'

So much has been done at this club and yet you get people, like the fanzine, and all they want to do is have a go. It was the same at Swinton. We won three trophies in five years but if we lost they bloody loved it, 'cos they could go in the pub or the club and say, 'Bloody told you, that manager's no good, that player's no good' and it's the same here. They love it when we lose because then they can go to their mates and say, 'What have I been bloody telling you?'

I feel let down when the players don't perform. Very much so. That is the reason I left Bolton. At the time I was on £120 a week, working 55 to 60 hours. Frank Worthington was on £500 to £600. Now I'm not saying Frank wasn't a fabulous player, but he worked 10 hours and if he did anything wrong, the spectators came in and had a go at Steve Walmsley and the rest of the staff, and the same applies here. I would also have to say that at this club there's not more than two or three players who earn more than the average working man.

Footballers, even those in the Premiership, are just ordinary people and talk to you like your mate in the pub. It's people at the top that have given them all this money, thousands a week, and created the £8 million footballer. If you got six football supporters off the terraces and put them in place of the directors, at any club, there would never have been a £1 million transfer, going back to Trevor Francis, and never have been players on thousands and thousands a week. The ordinary working man can't even think how much £1 million is, never mind £8 million.

Given his discontentment, you have to wonder why Walmsley, 11 years a divorcé and father of two teen-age daughters, doesn't get out of it. In the real world, however, it is not as simple as that. Perhaps it helps to wear his heart on his sleeve.

WALMSLEY
I've been wanting to get out for a long time, because things that have gone on have ripped the heart out of me and had me in tears. Too many years working too hard and too long have cost me – and put four stone on me. I've had no time for anything other than work. I've had a great time doing many happy things, but there are far *more* things I regret. I have worked from being 15½, and have worked every Saturday in that time.

There is not one more experienced person in the country doing what I do. That's why people ring me from everywhere for advice. Even some of the bigger clubs. I've been offered jobs at some top clubs, but they don't want to pay. They'll pay a footballer £12,000 a week, but let them pay the commercial manager £20,000 a year. I couldn't deal at the chief executive level of a top club. If there's one thing about me, I know my station.

Rochdale's players are contemplating an end-of-season holiday to Majorca as Docherty finalises his formation for the visit of Wigan's less celebrated team. Thackeray plants a brochure in front of his manager, indicating the preferred hotel, in Magaluf. He also says the lads would like day flights and are willing to pay the extra, rather than be thrown out of their hotel, many interminable hours before they are due at the airport. Like last year. This jaunt is their promised reward for making Anfield in the Cup. No one is suggesting they have their minds on the pool and the San Miguel, but something is weirdly amiss as the match unfolds. Peake plays a gentle back-pass to Key, who swings a leg, fails to make contact and turns to watch in horror as the ball rolls into the net. Whitehall has the chance to equalise from the penalty spot and, after nine out of nine this season, you would put Walmsley's profit on his scoring. Instead, he smacks the crossbar. Six minutes later, he has another penalty. You'd settle for nine out of ten and he has no hesitation about taking on the responsibility again. This time he blazes over. Thackeray concedes a penalty and Wigan lead 2–0. Dale spurn more chances, and the scoreline remains unchanged.

It is a tragicomic drama that encapsulates Rochdale's season. Perhaps their entire existence. For Whitehall, it is a personal farce, although he is as phlegmatic as ever.

'Just one of those things, isn't it?' (Two of those things to be precise, but anyway.) 'I had no doubts about taking the second one – and won't about taking the next one, either.'

Docherty defiantly insists a play-off place is not a lost cause, but others see it differently. 'That's our season over,' one says. 'It was a joke, an absolute joke.'

Except no one is laughing.

CHAPTER THIRTEEN

Paradise Lost

Monday morning as only Monday morning can be: bleak, grey, soulless. And this is the last Monday morning in March. Spring refuses to spring, buds and daffodils hunch tightly in wait for the sun's welcoming embrace. If hope is to spring eternal in the human breast, here is a real test. Promotion ambitions have been dismantled, piece by piece, and personal dreams shattered. Spotland, this Monday morning, is a vision of paradise lost.

The absence of players, given the day off, somehow deepens the sense of hopelessness; of a barren, abandoned wilderness. It also feeds a mood of frustration and dissension.

'Imagine what the fans would say if they knew,' cries a voice from the wilderness. 'They've got to go to work. They don't get a day off after a bad 'un. The players should be in now having shooting practice. Two penalties, loads of other chances missed – they should be working to put that right.'

Docherty is conscious he risks such criticism and faces it square-on.

DOCHERTY
We've not got a midweek game and with a congested programme ahead of us I believe I will get more out of the players by giving them this last chance of a long weekend's rest. We've got plenty of time to work on things during the week, don't worry about that. The players are fit. The important thing is to keep them as fresh as possible. I also know I cannot concede all hope is lost. I'm not giving it up. We could still win seven matches. I owe it to the players not to give up. We still have time.

There is not so much time, however, for transfer activity. The deadline is on Thursday and although Rochdale are in no position to go out and buy, they would have to be interested in any proposition to sell. Among those busy in the market are Preston, who spend £200,000 on Tranmere's Gary Bennett, a player Docherty inquired about a few weeks ago, when he sought a striker on loan. A non-League club splash £85,000 on a player. Come Thursday evening, the till at Spotland is still silent.

'Not a sniff,' Docherty says. 'Williams has gone to Doncaster on loan, so the board will be pleased we've saved a few bob there, but not even a call about Butler, Peake, Whitey – any of them.'

Docherty was expecting to be without Butler this weekend following the death of his mother, but he is intent on playing. 'Paul says he wants to play and dedicate the game to his mum,' the manager reveals. 'You can't buy that.'

Paul Adams is one of those told they will not be Rochdale players next season. At 18 and after two years on the

YTS scheme, he is to be another name on those ever-lengthening lists circulated by the League and the PFA.

Jimmy Robson was consulted by Docherty in the decision-making process.

ROBSON
Adams has got ability, he's good at running at people and going past them, but he doesn't tackle or win it in the air, so the play tends to go past him. He doesn't get involved as much as he should. The trouble is we have so few places and we have to look at the lads above him, the likes of Lyons and Taylor, and ask if he's going to be better and replace them in midfield. You can't honestly say that he is. It's hard and no one likes to do it, but decisions like this have to be made.

Paul is better known at the club as Eddie – yes, he is Young Eddie – a name that stuck after his spiked hair gave him the resemblance of a character from The Munsters. He lives with his parents, Frank and Sandra, in an end-of-terrace house on the main road from Rochdale to Milnrow and a junction of the M62. It is a neat, comfortable home, bearing the unmistakable touch of a house-proud wife and mother.

Patently, Sandra and Frank Adams have lavished much attention on the footballing aspirations of their only child. It is the classic scenario: outstanding schoolboy player, driven only by the desire to be a footballer and doting parents convinced he has the talent to make it. The feedback reinforced their conviction. Reviews from his matches under Rochdale's Centre of Excellence banner and even from the early part of the season suggested he was on course to becoming a fully fledged professional. And then the bombshell, a career off the rails. And now a family in emotional turmoil.

This Thursday evening Paul sits at the dining room table, his hands clasped before him, and talks quietly, at times almost in whispers, about his football life.

ADAMS

I've been with Rochdale since I was 14, as a schoolboy. All I wanted to do was to play football, and that's still all I want to do. When I was accepted on the YTS scheme I thought I was on my way. Jimmy always said I had a chance and I thought I was doing all right. But I've been injured for about four months. I've had groin trouble and struggled a bit. Recently they've been playing the young lads in the reserves, but being injured I've not had the chance.

Mick and Jimmy said they couldn't afford to take me on. He's got to cut his pros down to 16 or 17 next year. If he says he can't afford it, he can't afford it, but it's no consolation. A lot of the lads thought I'd get taken on. The senior players have been very good and sympathetic. A lot of them have been around a bit so they know people in the game and hopefully they can put me in touch with other clubs. Your name gets sent round to every club, anyway. I'll still try to get a League club, if I can, but if I have to go down to non-League then I will.

I still feel I can make it as a footballer. It's knocked my confidence a bit, but I still feel I can do it. It's all I've done since I left school. I've done leisure and tourism at college, but I want to carry on doing what I've been doing.

Frank Adams is a customer services manager who still plays local football.

ADAMS' FATHER
It was certainly a gamble for Paul to go into football, but it's a risk I think he'd got to take, for his own sake. What's happened to him just lately has upset the lad and it's upset us as well. He's had two years, and unfortunately it's come to a halt at the moment.

Initially I said we'd go to Rochdale because they were more likely to give him a chance. He was being watched by other clubs and the day before he signed, a scout asked him for his name and address, but we don't know where he was from. I thought that at Rochdale he would get noticed more. The downside is they have so little money and so few places.

I'm bitter because he's been injured so long and his second year has been a waste of time. At the beginning of the season he was going really well, and everybody down there obviously felt the same. Jimmy Robson kept coming to me and saying, 'Your Paul's really doing well.' Other people who saw him in A-team games said the same. He went to a specialist, eventually, and he's had a long rest. I'll encourage him now to get fit and keep trying, to give him his chance. I don't believe that's the end of it. I hope not, for his sake. We'll give it another try.

Sandra, a hairdressers' receptionist, is fretful in the way mothers are.

ADAMS' MOTHER
I definitely think he should keep trying, but I want it doing there and then. I'm worrying all the time. I can't switch off from it. I think they've been very unfair to him. Up to him being injured, they told him he was so close to getting a contract, and then all of a sudden . . . My husband won't let me go in and tell them what I think.

ADAMS
Jimmy told me I was letting myself down because I wasn't doing enough in the matches, but I wasn't training during the week, I was just playing on the Saturday. When everyone else is training, day in, day out, getting fit, I'm doing nothing, just resting. And he was expecting me to perform on Saturday. Sixty minutes into a game I was sore and tired. I got pains with every step. I realised that at Christmas time I had to start playing again. I wasn't fit but I had to.

ADAMS' FATHER
I spoke to Jimmy about that. On one occasion he came to me after a game and said, 'Your Paul, great skills, good passer, good shot, got nearly everything, but he doesn't work hard enough.' I got annoyed at that. I told him, 'You've asked him to play on Saturday, he's got a groin problem, which he's had now for three months, and you've done

nothing about it. All these other lads are super fit and you can't expect him to be able to run up and down the park all day long without training. It's not a problem when he's got the ball, but these lads just run right over him.

ADAMS' MOTHER
And it wasn't nice the way they told him. They'd told him on the Friday they were going to tell him on the Monday, so he'd all weekend to think about it. On the Monday he came home and said Doc had to go to sign Lancaster. So they didn't tell him until Tuesday night.

ADAMS
They made us sit through the Torquay game and then took us down, the apprentices, one by one, to the office and told us face to face. Jimmy and Doc were there. I just walked in, they told me to sit down, and Mick said, 'Eddie, we're not looking to take you on. We can't really do it because of the financial aspect.' It was quite upsetting. It was always going to be 50–50. [His father reckons it was 90–10 earlier in the season.]

There were six of us and they're keeping on two, but another one has been injured all year, so they take him out of the YTS scheme and have to give him an extension. The lads being kept on are both full-backs. He said they'd got players in midfield and I knew that, but Doc said that from what he'd seen of me this year I wasn't doing enough, I wasn't tracking back. To be honest, he's no right to say that because he's watched me in one youth game and seen me for 20 minutes in the reserves.

They've said they'll give me a reference and I'll write myself. You get a trial wherever you write. I'm not bothered where I go or whether I have to travel. Andy Thackeray says he can get me a trial at Torquay. If Peter Valentine gets a coaching job maybe he'll be able to get me something. I'll go anywhere.

ADAMS' MOTHER

I feel really hurt and bitter because I think he's been hard done by, but now we've got to look to the future. We'll do everything we can for him. I mean, that's all he's ever done. How many times did you go to Bobby Charlton's Soccer School? He went when he was seven. He won through to a school competition at Old Trafford.

Frank: 'Yes, the thing now is to look forward and I've told him, if we've got to go to Torquay, we'll go to Torquay. How we get there is not a problem as far as I'm concerned.'

Despite the ultimate disappointment, Young Eddie will take with him fond memories of Spotland, with all its menial tasks, the fetching and carrying, the kangaroo courts and all.

ADAMS

Well, that's all part of being an apprentice, isn't it? You have to go through that. I didn't mind the court thing. Besides, when Butler says you've got to do a forfeit, you do it. It was snowing when they made me run round the pitch with nothing on . . . I put my santa hat on and just got on with it. We've had a lot of fun. I've enjoyed it. Football's a good life.

Peter Valentine thinks football is a good life, too. It is all he knows, and he is approaching 33. Recurring knee trouble is curtailing his playing career, but he anticipated being appointed Rochdale's first team coach. Instead, he has been told the club cannot afford to create such a job. So, like Paul Adams, he is looking for work. Young or old, the plight and emotions are much the same.

As the rest of the players head for Lenny Barn – the advent of summer rugby league means Spotland is again out of bounds for training – Valentine goes through a solo loosening, stretching and exercising routine along the touchline of the not-to-be-trodden pitch. Unbeknown to him this Friday morning, Docherty is planning to call on his experience rather than the youthfulness of Bayliss, for tomorrow's home match against promotion candidates Gillingham.

His brief work-out completed, Valentine sits on the away team bench and, to the accompaniment of the groundsman's gently chugging roller, he talks about his football life.

VALENTINE
It was a big blow to be told I wouldn't be getting a job because I was made certain promises. The manager made promises and at the time he made them, I honestly thought he could deliver them. He'd asked me to take a cut in wages, which I was willing to do because you don't get paid the same

for being a coach as you do for being a player, and he said I'd have to work on a week-to-week contract, because that's all the manager's got. I told him that if that was what he was on and I was going to work for him, then obviously I'd do the same. It was just a question then of seeing the chairman about how much they were going to pay me.

Two days before I was supposed to see him, they had a board meeting and the Doc came back and said that because of financial reasons they're going to cut the staff next year, and because they're going to cut the staff, they don't need a first-team coach, so the job I was promised went out of the window. If he hadn't made any promises, it wouldn't have been so bad.

It all started when I asked the Doc if I could do some coaching, just to keep my hand in. I passed my full badge last summer. He said I could, and it went on from there. I get on well with the players, and the Doc and I seem to work well together. He then came up with the idea of my being first-team coach, which was a bonus for me because there's only so many coaches in the Football League, and it was as if I'd got my foot on the ladder. Then, three months later, the chairman knocks my foot off the ladder.

I could have joined Dave Sutton at Chorley to the end of the season, but he wanted me more as a player than a coach, and I did say to him I was looking for a player-coach or just a coaching job. But to be fair, if Rochdale could have sorted my contract out and paid me the money I was due, I would have gone to Chorley because Dave Sutton made me a good offer. But then we get Paul Butler and Dave Bayliss suspended, so the manager's had to turn me down on that one, as well.

The Doc's been really good to me because I've not been able to train properly for months. I play when he wants me to. Tomorrow, I don't know. It depends on how Paul Butler is. He's saying his mam would have wanted him to play, and that could just make his mind up. So if he's going to play Paul and Dave Bayliss that's not a problem. We've discussed that situation and I've just said I'll keep myself fit and if he needs me I'm available, because I'm still under contract until the end of June.

Valentine, a Yorkshireman, is the archetypal lower division, journeyman footballer. He also strikes you as a thoroughly decent man. He began playing with his local club, Huddersfield, and moved on, through Bolton, Bury and Carlisle to Rochdale. He lives in Wakefield with his wife, baby son and stepdaughter. And come the end of July, he could be out of work.

VALENTINE

If I don't get something else by then, basically I'm on the dole. I mean, that's what it boils down to. I took my coaching badge to stay in football, and if there's no job going in League football I'm going to turn to the non-League scene, and if there's nothing doing and I can't get a job in football, I'm going to have to go out and look for work. But to be honest, all I've ever done since I was 16 is play football. So it's going to be a tester.

I did a business course, but it was like being back

at school. It's not as if I could now walk into an office and say, 'Give me a job in business' because the course was not that advanced. I'm the sort of person who's willing to learn, but it's getting somewhere. I want to do something with the rest of my life, but employers now can get 16- and 17-year-old kids and pay them peanuts. I go in as a 33-year-old, used to a reasonable standard of living for the last 17 years, and if they offer me £100 a week to start learning something, it's going to be very difficult.

It's getting harder for kids coming into football now, especially in the lower leagues, because again, it's all down to finance. But I look at it like this: if you get a chance to play football when you're young, take it, because if you try it for two years and fail, then you've got to go out and get a job. If you haven't taken that chance, you've still got to get a job at 17. I could have been looking for a job at 16, but I managed to get into football. All I've done for 17 years is play football, so to me it has worked.

I've only ever played in the lower leagues, but I've made a living out of it, and I've got a house that's nicely in order. I've been advised to put a lot of money in a pension, which I've done, so in two years' time, through that and what you get through the PFA, I'll be fairly comfortable. But for the next two years I'm going to have to pull in the purse strings a bit.

If I could be a player-coach, or could get just a coaching job at a non-League club, and they could pay me X amount of pounds that I could live on comfortably for the next couple of years, then I'll

be happy with that. And you never know, if you get
into the Vauxhall Conference you could be back in the
League within a couple of years, and then I could pit
my wits against the Doc and the rest of them.

I'm big enough to admit, though, that if nothing
comes within the next four months, I'm going to
have to look elsewhere. I understand the financial
problems in football but you never think the day is
going to come when you face the end. When I was
young, older players used to say to me 'One day
you're going to have to retire', and I used to think,
'I'm only 26, I've got plenty of time.' All of a sudden,
I'm 32, and although I'm not ancient, because I've
got a bit of trouble with my right knee, I'm having
to face the end.

It's a bit of arthritis, wear and tear over the years.
I lost my fluid at a very early age and I've had
bone on bone for a lot of years, and if I do keep
playing I could do myself permanent damage. I
think football is important, but so is your health,
and your family, your wife and kids. So if I call it
a day at the end of this year, after 17 years, playing
in nearly 600 League and Cup games, I'll have had
a decent career.

I've certainly no regrets about coming into football and I would encourage Young Eddie to keep
trying. All I wanted was to play football so I can
understand how he feels. The game has got a lot
quicker, even in the lower leagues. When you look
at the Premier League, it's frightening. I know I lack
pace and when the opposition play the ball over the
top I've got no chance.

Funnily enough, though, I've played against Les

Ferdinand three times and always seemed to do well against him. But then I had a nightmare against John Barnes at Liverpool. Despite that, it was still one of the highlights of my career. Well, running out at Anfield, anyway. And I suppose I can say I scored there, even if it was an own goal. I've also played at Old Trafford, when I was with Bury. My biggest disappointment is that I've never played at Wembley, especially as I've been within 90 minutes of getting there half a dozen times. I've been that close in play-offs and knockout competitions in the lower leagues.

I suppose things have changed over the years, and that includes the players. The loyalty seems to have gone. People move on after two years to get a better deal. When I was younger, money didn't come into it. I had eight years at Bury. It was only when I was about 26 that I started thinking of my future. Players now think more about good moves that are likely to earn them decent money. I think the drugs thing is part of this. Tests show that some players have been taking performance-enhancing drugs. I suppose that's down to the pressure some feel. I've never been into enhancing drugs. In fact, I've never had a smoke. I like a pint. That's my weakness.

There's no point looking back, though, is there? I could sit and sulk and think this or that might have happened. If it wasn't for my knee trouble, who knows? But that's an occupational hazard. We all know that from the start. The important thing is to live for today and tomorrow. The likes of Young Eddie, they've got their whole lives in front of them.

And now I've reached the time of my career where I'm going to have to stop playing, I still feel I've got a lot to give to the game and that I can have a future in it.

The groundsman is still chugging up and down the pitch as Valentine's eyes scan Spotland and his resigned expression sums up his thoughts on Rochdale's future.

VALENTINE
If Doc gets promotion next season with 16 players he will deserve a job at a big club. But it's a joke, really. We've seen this season, with the injuries we've had, what can happen. You can imagine the situation next season. There's no proper training facilities here – they don't even have their own goals that they can move around. It's embarrassing. The thing that keeps a club like this going is the team spirit. It's all that's left.

Valentine's playing career lasts barely five more minutes. The early exertions in a match against Gillingham are more than the old knee can endure and he is forced to bid a sad farewell. Bayliss takes over alongside Butler only to injure an ankle and miss the second half. Deary drops back, inspires the resistance, and Rochdale retain the advantage of first-half goals by Stuart and Thompson.

Docherty's satisfaction with the result and the resourcefulness of his players is tempered by the realisation that Valentine will not play again. 'That's it, period. It's a shame he couldn't have played out the season, but Peter knew he was on borrowed time. Injuries, unfortunately, are part of the game, as a few of us have discovered to our

217

cost. A specialist broke the news to me by asking "Can you play the violin?" Then he introduced me to a dram.'

The manager also finally acknowledges that the promotion fantasy is over after his depleted team lose 1–0 at Colchester, and then 2–1 at Cambridge. 'We've no chance of making the play-offs now, we know that. It's disappointing after we were going so well earlier in the season and we've tried to cling on, but it wasn't to be.'

Injuries and suspensions have taken an inevitable toll and it says much about the club's predicament that Deary's two-match ban and £75 fine are greeted with mild celebration. They had feared he would be out for five matches. That does not, however, help Docherty in his selection for Easter Monday's home fixture with Barnet. More youngsters are in the equation and even Paul Moulden is back in the senior squad. Time for another rallying call from the manager.

DOCHERTY
I've told the players I don't want to see them taper away in the last few matches. We've still got our professional pride to play for and if they think they can pedal out the season at a gentle pace they can think again. The punters demand a performance and quite rightly so. It shouldn't be a problem being up for any match. If I play dominoes I play to win. It's the only way I know, the way it should be.

On paper, Barnet are a form team and we are really down to the bones as far as our squad is concerned. We're struggling to put together 14 fit players for this match. But they've had only four away wins this season so that suggests they don't travel too well, and if we give it everything, show the spirit we know is here, then we are quite capable of giving our supporters something to cheer about.

That optimism evaporates just 16 seconds into the match. Teenage defender Neil Barlow, called up for his full debut, fails to intercept an unexceptional pass and Lee Hodges gallops clear to score for Barnet. Within five minutes Barlow has physical injury to add to the mental bruises and is mercifully withdrawn. Dale contain Barnet for the rest of the first half but Hodges scores three more goals in seven minutes midway through the second half and Docherty's bedraggled troops retreat to that tormenting refrain: 'What a load of rubbish'.

It has all come to this.

CHAPTER FOURTEEN

Spoken from the Heart

With pernicious timing, fate has thrown the board and management of Rochdale AFC to the mob just three days after their demise reached new depths, the abysmal showing at home to Barnet. Planned some weeks earlier, this is the day the club opens its doors to the people. Youngsters, some 50 of them, with their parents, meet the players and watch them train. That's the easy part for Dale. It is likely to be different when the grown-ups have their chance in the evening, at a fans' forum, and they gather in force. The kick-off is delayed some ten minutes to give supporters ample opportunity to buy their beer.

Steve Walmsley is not unhappy about the delay. 'Don't let them sit down till we've sold all those scratch-off tickets,' he urges.

Graham Morris is characteristically apprehensive. 'Look at this lot – and I don't think they're here to say "Well done",' he suggests to Mick Docherty through a thin grin.

But then the manager has come prepared and he pointedly orders an orange juice. So has the chairman and he orders a pint. Walmsley reckons 200-plus are crammed into Spotland's main lounge as Les Duckworth, a veteran of these campaigns, calls the meeting to order and immediately adopts a defiant stance, refuting a rumour, aired in the *Manchester Evening News*, that boardroom resignations are imminent. Maintaining the aggressive tone, he invites the first question – to silence. 'No questions? That's it, then. Let's all go home.'

Yes, he's seen it, done it all before, and he uses the classic formula: address them in a confident, loud, positive voice, and put them on the back foot. The supporters are duly intimidated. Eventually one musters the courage to ask a question about the new stand. He is assured the building work will go ahead, but there are still problems over money and Hornets and so on. The gentle sparring continues with inquiries about the pitch and the hammering it is likely to take from summer rugby. Hornets, however, are to play only away games for a five-week period, to allow the grass to grow.

Eventually an elderly, white-haired, bespectacled man takes it upon himself to fire the first real salvo. The first two, in fact. 'Are the directors financially capable of running the club and will we have a new manager next season?' he demands to know.

'Yes and no,' Kilpatrick retorts.

'In what order?' the elderly man comes back.

Kilpatrick realises a little diplomacy is called for. 'I won't be flippant,' he says. Instead he draws on a touch of sarcasm to emphasise the thanklessness of his task. 'I've been trampled on by people wanting to get over me to this job. I've been fighting them off. I offered my 12,500 shares to Tommy Cannon for £1 – the lot – and he thought that was a bit much.'

The elderly man is tenacious, too. 'I've been coming for

62 years. My son comes and my grandson comes. And all we've seen is mediocrity.'

'Can't argue with that,' agrees Kilpatrick, 'but I believe we have gone forward, within the confines of the money we have. When I came here, staying out of the bottom four was the priority. Now we are aspiring to the promotion places. I know it's been bloody slow, but I do believe it's progress.'

Docherty is brought to his feet to explain some of his signings – Shaw, Williams, Lancaster and Thackeray, who one fan condemned as 'the worst full-back in the League'.

That stirs the mob and Docherty answers, 'I'm here all night and you can fire as many bullets at me as you can . . . A better pro you couldn't come across than Thackeray, limited though he is . . . I would love to be able to buy four, five, six good players . . . It's a fine balancing act . . . We were the best side in the bloody division till November.'

Moulden, one of the club's Lord Lucans – Shaw being the other – is mentioned and brushed aside again. 'Since Lancaster's been here, some of the weight has been taken off Whitehall,' Docherty reasons.

Another fan takes up the money theme again. 'When we played Darlington in the Cup and got Liverpool in the next round, we were near the top, so why was there no money given to the manager then? We never buy when we are at the top. We wait till we go down and buy deadlegs that can't get into other teams.'

'I would *like* to have bought then.'

Morris steps in: 'At the time, Mick didn't ask for money. We would have found it.'

But how much money? Docherty reminds the supporters that the likes of Preston, Gillingham, Bury and Wigan have their 'godfathers' and the means to spend vast amounts. 'I don't doubt if I had £500,000, even £300,000, I'd get Rochdale where they want to be. I have no doubts in my ability. Our goalkeeper cost only £20,000. I've had 14 players out, six for the rest of the season. In 29 years in football, I've never come across a situation like this.'

We return to Liverpool, where, as Docherty concedes, 'the floodgates opened in the second half'.

The elderly man strikes again. 'That's down to poor coaching, sitting back and letting them come at you.'

Docherty, now warming to the challenge, turns up the volume: 'There were 6,000 of you there that day – where are you now?'

The elderly man stands and points a finger at Docherty as he says: 'You've got no idea as far as I'm concerned.'

'You're entitled to your opinion,' retorts Docherty.

Kilpatrick deflects more sniping with the unfailing tactic of throwing open the boardroom door. 'If I have a serious offer for my shares, you can be sure I will sell them. I'm not going to spend the next 16 years of my life like the last 16 years, to finish up in a situation where I'm just being slagged off. If Tommy Cannon had been left at this club you probably wouldn't be here now – houses would be here now. We've saved it, we've developed it, and if anyone wants to take it on, it's there for the taking. I want to make that bloody clear.'

Docherty is in the fans' sights again. Why is Taylor playing midfield instead of up front?

'Because he's not strong enough to play that position.'

'Why has Moulden been ignored?'

'Because he's not good enough.'

That has the effect of a hand grenade, and the mob retaliate.

'Okay, okay, this is why we are here tonight,' Docherty shouts back. 'It boils down to my decisions. I'm trying to do the best I can. With a full squad I wouldn't have had to play Moulden. On Monday you were singing "What a load of rubbish" and I agree, but with so many players out I've got problems. The thing is the players didn't chuck it. They've had a lot to contend with, playing in foreign positions a lot of them.'

One fan makes the point that Docherty would have more options if Deary wasn't always suspended.

'But for 25 grand you'll never come across a better buy here.'

Another fan queries why Docherty took off Lyons and switched Whitehall to left-back the other day.

'Lyons played well, yes, but he was knackered. He was breathing out of his backside. It takes time for kids to come through. They aren't all ready. But hopefully we can get one good one through each year, like Butler, Bayliss and Price. That's why we've got a youth policy . . . People are calling for my head, but that goes with the territory. You can say my best isn't good enough but it won't be for the want of trying. I hold my hands up and say Shaw was a mistake.'

Francis Collins, from the fanzine, wearing his black and green away shirt, gets to his feet to suitable acknowledgement from the panel and the floor. Jeers there may be, and condemn him they might (a number of fellow fans threatened to throw him over the wall at Chesterfield), but he commands attention and respect. Club officials, including the chairman, manager and commercial manager, welcomed him earlier with first-name greetings and expansive smiles. All of which he must find deeply amusing and satisfying.

'Francis' is invited to put his question, which amounts to an inquiry-cum-statement that unless Docherty has a squad of first-team-calibre players after his 'clear-out', nothing will change next season.

'Excellent question, Francis,' replies Docherty. 'Didn't think you had it in you.' He confirms there will be a 'clear-out' at the end of this season and that it is his intention to ensure 'quality' through his squad. He admits, however, that the likes of Butler and Peake will be in no hurry to accept new terms in case they receive better offers. 'They could sit on it until July, and that's no good to me. The probability is that they will want to go elsewhere, and then we've got problems.'

Jimmy Robson, a statesman-like figure in the stump-type atmosphere of the evening, interjects, and when the man who scored the 100th FA Cup final goal at Wembley does so, people listen. 'I have my ideas on why things have gone wrong. Everybody points their finger at the goalkeeper situation, which is right, but I also thought the left side of the team was very important, with Formby, Peake and Stuart. You had a good wing there, three tidy performances, quite subtle. Then, of course, we got Formby and Stuart injured. Down the right, with Thackeray and Thompson, we were more direct. It gave us a good mix. If we can get those three on the left together again next year we'll do as well as we did at the start of this season.'

Another veteran fan talks of his total and utter frustration. 'I've been coming 45 years, and to be honest we have been good in the last three seasons, we've been in the top three or five. But it looks like someone here, and this is what's being said –'

Kilpatrick is already smiling that irritated, dismissive

smile and as an aside says, 'I wonder what's coming now.'

The fan resumes: 'Well, this is what's being said – that somebody's fixed it.'

'I'm not even going to answer that,' says Kilpatrick, utter disdain now etched on his face.

Someone, inevitably, wants to know about Williams. Docherty informs him the player will be back from Doncaster when his loan spell is over and will be freed at the end of the season.

'Why not give him away now?'

'You can't *give* him away.'

Morris explains that no club need sign him until August because Rochdale are obliged to pay his wages until 31 July. Morris, however, has turned that situation to his club's advantage by blocking the signing of Lancaster until he formally splits with Bury.

'Sack him,' a voice implores.

'We can't sack him, either,' Morris says, ruefully.

Kilpatrick cannot resist a little mickey-taking. 'You've got to be fair to Williams: married to the daughter of a millionaire, villa in Spain, taking helicopter lessons . . . He did a deal with a club, that he could go on a month's loan and not ask for wages. No doubt he would borrow something off the missus. But he couldn't do it because it was illegal!'

'Sounds like he's the ideal person to take over this club, then,' an alert fan chimes in.

'But you signed him. Why?' asks another fan.

'*I'm* not answering that,' replies Kilpatrick.

Docherty, taking the hint, stands and says: 'You're bob on, sir. But if everybody got it right all the time it would be bloody boring. It would be lovely to have

£30 million or £40 million to go and buy the best players. At our level you've got to be right all the time. The board are backing the manager as best they can. I may have dropped one or two clangers, but it balances out and eventually when Gray moves on, it will pay for all the mistakes.'

'I'm not knocking you,' says one fan to Docherty. 'You've only been given £20,000. It's these fellows here who are not giving you the money.'

'We agree. We need money,' agrees Kilpatrick. 'Why wasn't Jack Walker born in Rochdale? Why is it this town doesn't produce multi-millionaires willing to spend their money on the club? Don't knock us, we've done our best. We've put securities with the bank for an overdraft of £100,000. If our best is not good enough, fine. I accept that. If we all have to resign tomorrow, no problem. I've had great times and made good friends through this club. But I'm not prepared to say I'll keep putting the money in. I've not got the money. I've got three children, three grandchildren and the Ayatollah at home, and she doesn't know I've put *anything* in!'

Docherty explains how he has to investigate the character of a player before signing him, to discover 'if he is into birds, booze, gambling – or all three.'

'Sign him,' the chairman butts in.

The double act has charmed some of the venom from the audience. It was always more subtle than warfare, more a game of chess, and Kilpatrick and Docherty, like Duckworth, are skilled players on this board. Now the resistance is muted. Another 'lifer' of 35 years shares the frustration of his fellow supporters, but applauds the work of the club in the schools and the community; he applauds the development of young players and

228

he applauds the very fact Rochdale still has a League club, unlike Newport, Halifax and a number of other towns.

Docherty gratefully accepts the accolades and diverts the credit for work with the youngsters and in the community to Dave Bywater and Keith Hicks, who are both beaming silently at the end of the table.

The now chummy feel is undisturbed by a complaint about the catering. 'The only good thing about coming here was the pies. They're nothing like what they were.'

Then, out of the blue, a potentially tricky one is voiced. Docherty is asked to run through the training schedule. Now much as he believes in his way of doing things, this may not be the time and place to mention that the players were excused work on Tuesday and Wednesday this week, or talk about the unorthodox forms of exercise. He does say that the programme varies, from the pre-season morning and afternoon sessions, to the less intense agenda later in the campaign, and that their training is often determined by the weather and, of course, a lack of facilities.

Docherty's silver tongue gets him out of that corner and he can relax as the board are drawn into debates about stewards, policing, and a membership scheme.

'We've got a degree in cock-ups,' Kilpatrick confesses. 'But I'm adamant that a membership scheme would be good for home supporters and for the club, who would then be in a position to take more at the gate from visiting fans.'

Francis is in *enfant terrible* mode again, storming the Bastille with: 'If the board put a membership scheme in place they will be guilty of betraying the fans.'

It seems the old Thatcherite stigma cannot be erased.

229

The concept of an identity card is perceived as an infringement of civil liberties. Kilpatrick is beside himself: 'We're actually trying to save you money. We're not trying to get money out of you. Hell fire.'

Francis is on the rampage. He is not satisfied that Docherty said he would have a squad of quality players. 'Are we over-expectant in wanting promotion?'

'I would have said at the start of the season that the expectation was there and had we gone past Christmas in contention I would have been thinking on those lines,' replies Docherty. 'But I don't want to tempt fate and leave us with egg on our faces. I'm confident that the 16 to 18 players will get us where we want to be.'

It is common knowledge Valentine was lined up as first-team coach and Docherty admits: 'Maybe I led Peter up the garden path a bit. But if I'm working on 16 to 18 players, his wage would be better spent on a player. It's cruel, it's hard, it's cynical, but that's the way we had to look at it.'

A fan towards the back introduces himself as a referee.

'Can you see me from there?' Docherty asks.

The referee rides the comment, as referees do, and puts it to Docherty that he might tighten the disciplinary rein, offering Brian Clough's exemplary regime at Nottingham Forest as the standard he should aspire to.

'I've fined only two for dissent this season, so we've done well there,' Docherty replies. 'Well, I fined Formby after he was sent off at Torquay. Deary was for dissent. Fifty per cent of the bookings, I believe, have been unwarranted.'

Two and a half hours into the evening, Kilpatrick embarks on his closing speech. 'It's been mega-frustration this year. People talked at the start of the season about Vauxhall Conference, that we'd no hope, and we turned that around superbly well. It was a joy to watch us in some of those early games, against Hartlepool, and Exeter, and Darlington, and Rotherham, and when you contrast that with some of the more recent performances, well, really, we understand how you feel. But *we* also feel it. The fates have conspired against us and I think the Wigan game summed it up. I couldn't believe so much could go wrong. It encapsulated our season.

'The board will not stand in the way of development. This is not a private little club. But we have a responsibility to maintain the running of the club, and no way is anyone going to walk away from it. Hopefully we can put someone on the board to give it a tremendous boost, but an indication of the feeling for the club is the numbers in which you have turned up tonight. Points you raised have been made before – privately, to Michael. We know what you are thinking because we are fans, just the same as you.'

The chairman also wishes to show the other, more acceptable face of 'selfish, money-grabbing' footballers, relating their willingness to attend the funeral of the 17-year-old girl. 'I thought that was superb. It's about caring for the community, and why we've tried to keep that going, because it's so important to us all.'

Generous applause confirms a personal success for Kilpatrick.

Duckworth attempts the last word: 'That's why we're here. We all love this club.'

A lone voice from the audience denies him with 'Up the Dale.'

*　　*　　*

Rochdale have, in football parlance, a 'result' to bolster them through these torrid times and the return of principal players revives a sense of purpose through preparations for the visit to Chester. Butler, Bayliss and Deary are all available again after completing suspensions. Nothing, however, could have prepared Docherty and his team for the drama to come.

Dale recover from an early penalty by Darren Ryan, the player they sacked, to take command against the team who outclassed them earlier in the season, with two assured goals by Whitehall. But this is scarcely the half of it.

With time slipping away, the ball goes out of play for a throw-in and Taylor, sitting on the bench, flicks it away rather than feed eager Chester arms. Peter Jackson, captain of the home team, is incensed and swings a boot at Taylor's midriff. Jackson is sent off and his manager, Kevin Ratcliffe, so composed and urbane at Spotland, takes over the mantle of the raging bull and confronts Docherty. Arms flail and Lancaster, another of the substitutes, emerges from the melee, gripping Ratcliffe, who is further restrained by police. The match completes its course, a 2–1 win to Rochdale.

Behind the scenes, the two managers come together again and, over a drink, pragmatism prevails. Docherty is aware that his player was in the wrong and that his team have three points.

Ratcliffe, rendered vulnerable by the realisation that his previously imperious side may now miss the play-off cut, is equally conscious that unless he is contrite and does a quick patch-up he could be hauled before the FA. He tells the Press, 'It was a heat-of-the-moment thing. Tensions are high because we've got a lot to play for.'

Docherty says: 'Ratcliffe lost it and if Lanky hadn't dragged him off there might have been trouble. But then we had a chat and he apologised and that's it as far as I'm concerned. It happens. It's a passionate game. There's a lot of tension on the bench and he knows how important this match was for his club. I always seem to be involved in something at this place. I got sent off two years ago.'

Another grey afternoon, another trip. This time to Mansfield. Players in blue and white tracksuits mingle in the reception area. Docherty, in shirt and tie, pops out for a sandwich and returns to organise the skips.

Les Duckworth, occupying his hatch, inquires: 'Do you want your hands bandaging? Oh, and don't forget your gumshield.'

Directors have been going down like British heavyweights, the chairman is making his own way to the match from work and Graham Morris is away, so there are plenty of spaces at the front of the bus. Rochdale have a stand-in physio because John Dawson has damaged his back falling off a push-bike, but they also have an experienced doctor and a familiar figure occupying a new role. Keith Clegg, just appointed managing director, sits in the position of tour leader.

As the bus pulls up outside the main entrance at Mansfield Town FC, Docherty stands, turns his head towards the players and announces: 'Same team, same subs, same numbers.' What a luxury.

The pitch, too, is a change for the better. Plenty of grass, soft enough to take a stud. There is a more comfortable feeling within the camp. A good win can have that effect. It is as if they are released from the pressures of success and failure. Managers often say it yet can rarely mean it:

Enjoy it. That, however, appears to be entirely possible this evening.

Whitehall is brushing his boots, paying particular attention to the left. 'I get through three lefts to one right,' he mocks himself. He is sporting an in-vogue growth on his chin. 'It's my lucky beard. Got two with this on Saturday, so I'll have to keep it on while things are going well. I'll shave it off tomorrow.'

Andy King, no mean player in his time, now manager of Mansfield and still hyper-energised, pops his head in Rochdale's dressing room and asks for Docherty. They are old pals and disappear for a natter. Docherty returns to inform his players King has in his squad a 16-year-old wonderboy. One or two have heard something about him. His name? Ryan Williams. England under-17s.

The players drift out onto the pitch for a loosener, all except Deary, who goes through a routine of exercises in the dressing room. A sturdy, fearless figure, he says, 'I don't bother going out. I'd just mess around if I did. I can loosen up and do my stretching in here.'

His colleagues return to report their first sighting of the wonderboy. Unless they are confusing him with a ballboy or a mascot, he is a midget. 'You'll be able to tower over him, Jamie.'

A substantially larger being fills the doorway and, with a pained expression, asks for Dawson. It transpires that the chairman has done his back a mischief and presented an unlikely first task for the stand-in physio who apparently is called Steve, or Norm, or both. The young stand-in, a mite apprehensively, gives Kilpatrick a cursory examination and offers treatment tomorrow.

'What a load of bull,' a familiar voice chimes as the chairman makes for the door.

'I heard that, Deary,' Kilpatrick says, checking his stride.

'Sorry chairman, thought you'd gone.'

Deary is usually at the hub of the fun and he has an appreciative audience. The mood becomes more business like as Docherty issues his final instructions. He calls for total concentration, particularly early in the game, when recently the team have been conceding goals. He exhorts them to finish the season on a high, to have pride in their performance, as professionals, to express themselves and to enjoy it. Yes, there it is. They troop out in a barrage of mutual good wishes and would have you believe they are ready to take on the world. 'You can never tell,' Docherty guards.

He takes his place in a tiny dugout. The substitutes sit out in the drizzle. The resident character, a simpleton of advanced years, in a flat cap, leans over the terrace wall and pokes his head into the dugout to greet the visiting management and ask for autographs. He wants to know how many games Rochdale have left. The Doc tells him. He tells the Doc how many Mansfield have left and reels them off, home and away. When the Doc talks to Lancaster the man in the flat cap joins in the conversation.

If you are beginning to think the lunatics have taken over the asylum you might be convinced once the match is underway and King is on his feet, at the touchline, a cheroot in his right hand, bellowing instructions and profanities at his players. One denunciation is particularly memorable. The first three of four words are: 'You sloppy little . . .'

The simpleton in the flat cap leans over again: 'Leave him alone. You do your job.'

Docherty enjoys the cabaret. 'You can shout too much

because it reaches a point where the players don't listen, but in fairness he's all right.'

King, that is. He is certainly entertaining, Luton-born but sounding Cockney to anyone North of Watford, especially when yelling at the top of his voice. He is a natural for a bit part in *Minder* or *Only Fools and Horses*.

Not that he has too much to complain about in the opening exchanges. Mansfield are the more progressive, penetrative team, almost capitalising on Key's miskick, and being awarded a penalty when Martin, in a moment of unquestionably sound judgement, throws up his hands to prevent the risk of decapitation by a short-range missile. The referee, with a similarly swift response, blows his whistle and points to the spot. Martin's plea for the right of self-preservation cannot move him. 1–0 to Mansfield.

Just the start the Doc did not order, but his team, operating with Whitehall as the lone striker, tilt the balance of play towards half-time. Whitehall allows a chance to get away and appeals for handball in the area are ignored. 'Don't we get a penalty for that, ref?' Docherty wants to know.

Just before the interval, Martin is struck down after all. He is on the floor, clutching a knee, and anxious team-mates shout for attention. 'Have you got a doctor?' Docherty asks King.

Derek Hall runs towards the touchline to tell his manager that Martin is screaming.

Docherty instructs Taylor to get ready and tries to determine the extent of the damage. 'Medial ligament,' he is told by the doctor.

'He's not moved,' observes Lancaster.

'When you get those, you don't,' says Docherty. 'I've done both mine.'

Play is held up for three to four minutes as Martin's knee is strapped and he is carried off, to sympathetic applause. The rest soon follow him up the tunnel for the half-time break. Docherty grabs a tea from the dressing room and checks on his injured player. 'Just a tear,' is the latest bulletin. The players have news for him, claiming the referee admitted a mistake over the penalty. Next on the manager's agenda is a debate with Whitehall about his movement. The striker stands his ground – to no one's surprise – but does not give Docherty a serious problem. In fact, the manager would prefer more noise from the rest. 'Come on, it's a bit quiet,' he rallies. The bell is a signal to raise their voices and expectations again.

Despite the warnings, Rochdale start the second half as slowly as they started the first. Mansfield spring the offside trap and almost have another goal. Cometh the hour, cometh the wonderboy. He is, indeed, short, but very chunky, his head seemingly squashed into his shoulders, an appearance exaggerated by his cropped hair. An East Midlands Maradona? His first contribution is certainly ominous for Dale. He arrows the ball low from the left, to the near post, and Key has to get down smartly to field it.

Midway through the half Docherty, too, makes a sub-stitution, bringing on Lancaster for Taylor. The young-ster, his eyes ablaze in rage, shuns Docherty's attempt to usher him towards the bench and scurries up the tunnel. 'I'll have him for that,' the Doc says through clenched teeth.

His look is blacker still when Key pushes out a deflected shot and who should pounce but the wonderboy. 'Goal-keeping error,' Docherty groans.

Rochdale belatedly piece together their game and King

goes more public with his displeasure as Hall heads in from Whitehall's cross. An excellent goal and an even better one follows. This time Thompson is the supplier and Whitehall the finisher. Docherty leaps to his feet and turns his gaze on the stand behind, his expression of defiance a challenge to all-comers.

Now he is animated, sensing a win. Martin arrives at the dugout on crutches, keen for a resumé of what he's missed. A little boy, leaning over the terrace wall like the man in the flat cap, is more interested in the state of his health.

'What have you done?'

'Twisted my knee.'

Martin appears less distressed than the Mansfield defence, who are frantically trying to organise themselves as Deary prepares to launch a free-kick. 'Plenty of snow, Loafy,' Docherty encourages. 'Plenty of snow.'

Mansfield survive the snow storm and an even greater threat when Thompson's shot is deflected a couple of inches wide. From the corner, the goalkeeper manages a crucial, punched clearance. It is the final scare. Honours are even.

The players are still exchanging congratulations as they settle on the benches in the dressing room. Docherty adds his contribution to the buzz and singles out Hall for personal words of praise. But he brings a hush from the rest as he addresses the player who already has changed into his tracksuit, his head bowed.

'I do things for the benefit of the whole team, Jamie Taylor, not for you. LOOK AT ME WHEN I'M TALKING TO YOU. You go up the tunnel like that again and I'll fine you good and hard. Right lads, it's 9.35. We leave at 10? That all right?'

If it isn't nobody says.

'Ten it is.'

Docherty leaves Taylor to stew and the others to shower, and sets off on his regular post-match round. He pops into the boardroom, where the home club's sponsors, Mansfield Brewery, are being accorded due respect, gives an interview to Mike Brookes and looks in on King. By 10 o'clock the players are gathered outside the main entrance, some cradling Cornish pasties in their hands, and eventually they realise the bus is waiting for them at the far end of the car park. 'Where are the taxis?' Deary wonders aloud.

Taylor still is not smiling but has doubtless been given some advice by more experienced team-mates. On the bus, he sidles up to Docherty, and in a barely audible voice, apologises. Docherty accepts and holds out his hand. As they shake, the manager, also speaking softly now, says he knows the player is upset but that he must understand the manager's wider responsibilities. Taylor nods and returns to his pasty.

Docherty heads back up the M1 and across the M62, a contented manager. Behind him, the players, playing cards or just musing, are contented, too. Even Martin is at ease, assured that his injury is not complicated. Now beyond the sympathy stage, he is the butt of wise-cracks from Deary and company. As Thackeray and Stuart help him to his car at Hartshead Services, that familiar voice from the back booms: 'See where he's parked? In the disabled!'

CHAPTER FIFTEEN

New Life – New Hope

The last match, the next match, goals, injuries, other teams, other players: they talk shop here as they do in any other job. Also as in any other job, they talk comings and goings, mortgages, cars, holidays, schools. And they talk babies. This is a subject suddenly close to the heart for Jason Peake and Paul Butler, whose partners recently informed them they were to become fathers. To the undisguised amusement of their colleagues, Peake and Butler have been comparing notes and scans, the central defender even contemplating the possibility of being presented with twins.

For both young men this is an experience which eclipses football and all its trials, bringing life into context with burgeoning impact the way it does for all expectant parents. For Butler there is poignancy, too, the joy of new life helping him through the sadness of his mother's death – the essence, wonder and hope of nature.

Coincidentally, these are the two Rochdale players who reportedly have attracted most interest from scouts and are expected to have new clubs by the start of next season. Docherty has made them improved offers, but they are exercising their right to keep their options open. In every sense, they seek new life, new hope.

Peake, with blond hair, a delicate touch, good balance and vision, looks the part of a player meant for a grander stage. Indeed he appeared to be on his way when he won England Youth recognition and made the senior breakthrough with his local club, Leicester City. Instead, the journey took him to some of the English game's backwaters: to Hartlepool, on loan, to Halifax, and the Vauxhall Conference, and then, two seasons ago, to Rochdale. Here he has recovered his confidence and optimism, and would leave with mixed feelings.

PEAKE
It's confusing, really. Part of me wants to stay. They're a great bunch of lads and Doc's brought me on, made me a far better player. But I see some of my friends playing in higher divisions and in the Premier League, and I'm thinking, 'I'd like a crack at that.' I want to play as high as I can and better myself.

We all play for the love of the game, but we've also got families. I've got a baby on the way so I want to make as much money as I can while I'm in the game. It's a short career. This is our first baby and it's unbelievable. We went to this scan the other day and it changes your whole perspective on life; what are the important things and what are not. We're getting married in the summer, so I've got all this to think about.

[There might, of course, have been cause for double celebration, but Peake has no doubts why there isn't.] The club being in the financial situation they are. When we started getting the injuries to Ian Gray and Mark Stuart, unlike the Prestons, who could go out and replace them, we couldn't because we don't have the financial clout. Doc's done his best, we all did our best, but it wasn't to be. We weren't strong enough, simple as that. Money talks in football and we didn't have it to get us through that sticky two and a half months around Christmas.

Ultimately a player has to put his own future first, and this player has been conscious of the prying eyes.

PEAKE
Obviously it's flattering. You try not to think about it during a game but when you make a mistake you think, 'Is that going to be magnified and look ten times worse than it is?' At the end of the day you've just got to relax and try to do your best and do the things that attracted people in the first place, which I think I've maybe done.

We live in a lovely little place near Burnley and we're very happy there, but my roots are in Leicester and ideally I'd like to move closer to home. I'm an only child, very close to my parents, so I've found it hard being away from home, and it's their first grandchild and they want to see the baby as often as possible. If I can't go back to the Midlands I'd prefer to stay in the North-West. So I don't have to move.

No other club has spoken to me yet. The logical thing to do is sit on it and see. Doc knows the score. I think Paul will do the same thing. We talk about things because there's only a year between us and we're good friends. We pick each other's brains. He's a very good player and it will be amazing if he doesn't get away.

Dean Martin's injury at Mansfield is a further reminder of the precarious nature of this trade and serves to encourage any player to take what he can while he can.

PEAKE
During the next match I could have something happen to me and be out for who knows how long. Look at David Busst at Coventry. He would never have thought he'd get his leg so badly smashed at Man United and now the poor chap's out for 12 months and might never play again. It's bound to affect you when it's one of your own team-mates, one of your friends, who's hurt. We're a small club and we're all very close. Every week you read about bad injuries. There are lots of knees going and now hernias seem to be the trendy thing. It's frightening.

Regardless of the situation, though, I've got to do my best for Rochdale Football Club. They pay my wages. At the same time, if somebody offers them £200,000 for Jason Peake, would they turn it down? Knowing Doc, in his heart of hearts he'd want to turn it down, but would it be the thing to do for the club? It's good money for them.

I've done my best at left-back and quite enjoyed it. Doc knows where I want to play, but what's the point going on about it? Hopefully I've helped him out. I consider myself a midfield player but I've heard people say I'm better at left-back. I'm a footballer and these days you've got to be able to play anywhere, especially in our situation.

It's upset us as much as the fans that we've not been able to get promotion and now we can't be seen to be easing up. Their entrance fee hasn't been cut so we've got to keep up our performances and give them value for money. The diehards are always there. You see the same faces, and you know them, be it Exeter, Plymouth or Mansfield, in a match which, let's face it, didn't matter. But it's a round trip of about £30 with food and petrol, so they don't want to see us throw the towel in with four games to go.

Yes, you think they are a bunch of so-and-so's at times, when they are getting on to you, but then you think again and realise they are entitled to. Some of these fans may have been up at six to go to work and have still made it to the match, and then you know how lucky you are playing football.

My career has been like a ride on a roller-coaster. One minute you think you're a star, local lad doing well at Leicester, in the paper and everything. Twelve months later, Brian Little came, free transfer, Halifax Town, Vauxhall Conference, out of the Football League. Nobody thinks of you then, do they? It was absolutely horrendous at Halifax. The night we got relegated I took my troubles home, which I know wasn't fair on my girlfriend. But then Dave Sutton came in for me, which was a Godsend, and things have got better ever since. I got the chance to start again, at the bottom of the ladder, and you have to if you want to do well in the game.

I know a lot of people who've done well as kids and now you see them playing in the Conference because they've just given up. There's something inside me that says I can play at the highest level, I know I can, I still believe that. That's what's keeping me going. I've seen my mates playing at the top and I want to play there with them. I played with Paul Kitson, who's at Newcastle now, Des Lyttle, who's at Forest, Scott Oakes, now at Luton, Richard Smith, who's in Leicester's first team, and Julian Joachim, who's gone to Villa.

I know, deep down, I can be with them and it's a killer watching them on the telly because I know they got the breaks and I didn't. I know a friend of Gary Lineker, when he was at Leicester, and he was a better player than Lineker. When there were a couple of injuries in the first team Lineker got in for two or three games, scored a couple of goals and that was it. If my friend had got the chance instead, who knows where Gary Lineker might be now? Maybe selling fruit on Leicester market with his family. There's so much luck involved in football. But Lineker learned, used everything he had to the maximum and he's done brilliantly. You see him on the telly now and he's superb.

I think I am realistic and I've also thought what I might do outside the game, and I quite fancy chiropody. My girlfriend squirms at the thought but I don't mind. Much as I love football and want to stay in it I realise it is not the be all and end all. There are more important things in life. The baby, for a start. And football doesn't matter at all when you hear about some of the tragedies around us.

Dunblane really got to me. All those little kids. Any attacks on kids, and old folk, sicken me. Yes, we all want to do well on the football field, but let's keep it in perspective.

Butler was nurtured with less illustrious friends, right here at Spotland. A 23-year-old Mancunian, six foot two tall and with legs like small oaks, he has the presence of a formidable central defender and a deceptive turn of speed to break the heart of hopeful forwards. Few doubt the justification of his ambition and Sunderland, newly promoted to the Premiership, are among those who have been closely following his progress.

BUTLER
You play even better knowing scouts are watching you, but the team comes first. You play for the team and if you play well it's a bonus. No disrespect to Rochdale, but I want to play at a higher level, everyone does. They've given me the chance in football but there comes a time to move on. I've been here five years and for the past three years we've nearly got there and faded away. It disappoints you.

Of course Sunderland would appeal. Anyone in the Premiership would. Sunderland are going forward, building a new stadium, and I've got family up there, on my mother's side. Mind you, they're all Newcastle fans! Moving home is no problem. You've got to take that as it comes. Same with the ups and downs. My wife knew what she was letting herself in for when she married me. Sometimes I take my football home with me and she knows if I just sit there not to say anything. She's had that over the six years we've been together. Some days we talk about it, some we don't, it just depends what mood we're in. She comes in from work in a worse mood than me some days, so I'd rather not speak to her on those days. We have our arguments, but that's in all relationships.

It's incredible, though, what effect a baby can have on you and it's helped me a lot these last few weeks. It was funny both Jason and I came in within a week of each other and said the missus was pregnant and we've been keeping tabs on each other's situation ever since. One of the good things about a small club like this is that you tend to be closer, even down to the tea lady. You need that bond when you have such a small squad, and you become good mates.

I still see my old mates at home, when I go out at weekends, and it makes me remember we have a pretty easy life as footballers. They've been working from nine till nine some days and doing overtime. I'm getting home at half twelve, one o'clock every day and you shouldn't forget that. Hopefully you can make a good living out of it. I'm looking into PFA courses and over the next year or two I'll probably do something. But if I get a good move, it could set me up.

I've learned a lot at Rochdale and been lucky to play with some good centre-halves, like Alan Reeves, then Peter Valentine. Now it's down to me to pass on what I've learned to the likes of Dave Bayliss. I enjoy that responsibility. I've always thought of myself as being a bit of a leader and I've felt more and more that way.

Losing Peter was just one of the blows we've had, but we've knuckled down, played the YTS kids and got on with it without moaning. You hear some teams whingeing 'We've got five or six players out' but if they had what Doc's had they wouldn't be able to cope. You couldn't ask for a better bunch of lads than these. The kangaroo courts are all part of it. It's part of learning and the more the kids get involved with the first teamers the better. They know us as friends instead of looking up at us as if we don't like them. To give Doc his credit, he's always given kids a chance and he always will do.

Butler, having taken his chance, now aspires not only to the Premiership but also to the international arena – be it for England, Wales or the Republic of Ireland.

BUTLER
I'm English, my dad's side is Welsh and I've married into an Irish family. My wife came over from Ireland when she was seven. So I'm qualified for all three. I think you've got to be playing for one of the top clubs to be picked, and that's where I think it's wrong. I think they should be looking in the lower leagues. There are some players just as good. I don't know if the Irish and Welsh are aware I'm qualified, but they can ask, can't they?

Butler has the stall to advertise his wares in the home match against Scunthorpe. Deary's early goal gives Rochdale the initiative but Bayliss's dismissal, for hauling back an opponent just outside the area, leaves his fellow defenders to try to hold out for almost an hour. They succeed for

249

more than half that period before yielding an equaliser and the score stays at 1–1 to the end.

There is greater concern in some quarters about the outcome of a meeting the following Monday, with the manager. Docherty is to reveal his retained list, also naming those players he will not be keeping. Those given free transfers are: Clarke, Valentine, Shaw, Williams, Moulden, Hardy, Lyons, Proctor and Powell. Those offered new contracts are: Butler, Formby, Thompstone, Peake, Taylor, Thompson, Stuart and Russell. Lancaster has been lined up for next season but Docherty is still undecided about Hall. Gray, Bayliss, Thackeray, Deary, Martin and Whitehall are under contract.

Most had suspected their fate, but Clarke, the goalkeeper overlooked after Gray was injured, is devastated by the news. 'The lad is very upset and I can understand that,' Docherty says. 'But if I'm down to a squad of only 18 players I am going to have to operate with only one goalkeeper. As for the players offered terms, I can only wait and hope. If they all accept I'll be able to take on two more players in the summer.'

Clarke, ironically, will be recalled for the final match, at Hereford, because Key completes his loan period in Dale's last home fixture, against promotion-chasing Plymouth. The goalkeeper is beaten once, midway through the second half, and that is enough to claim the points as Dale, true to their character since those heady days, early in the season, spurn a series of chances. The campaign is tapering away in precisely the manner Docherty warned against, the annual awards evening ringing a little hollow. Butler, unsurprisingly, is the players' player of the year.

The end of the season will come as a relief. So will the

long and eagerly anticipated trip to Majorca. Much to the players' and Docherty's dismay, however, there appears to be a misunderstanding about the extent of the incentive offered for reaching that lucrative third-round tie. The board argue the sunshine pledge was intended only for the senior squad and not all the players. Or, in financial terms, a £5,000 bonus and not £7,500. Docherty tells his charges he is pulling out of the holiday by way of protest. 'Mind you, Thack's left my ticket on my desk and put me on the spot,' he says. 'But I want to make a point.'

The players agree to pay the difference to ensure no one is excluded. They also have the fines fund for spending money and that much-vaunted team spirit to draw upon.

Down in the dressing room, with the season's penultimate training session over, the oft-abused Thackeray is shouldering the captain's burden with characteristic diligence.

THACKERAY
This has soured the end of the season a bit because almost all the squad, including the younger lads, wanted to come away with us,' he says. 'But the players have stuck together, and if we have to spend our own money we will. I think there'll be 24 of us and a couple of staff.

We'll have a good trip. With us coming from various parts of the North we split up after matches and don't tend to socialise together on Saturday nights, but going away for a week like this, it's the male bonding situation, where you find out things about players you would never have dreamed, warts and all. When we have bad times next season we can look back on the holiday and I'm sure it will help us through.

Since I've been playing football, for 12 years, I've never missed a year with the lads. People ask me what I'm doing, still going away with the lads at 28 and what does my wife think about it. I say that to be fair it's nothing to do with my wife. She's quite happy with the situation and likewise, if she said she was going away with all her workmates I wouldn't have a problem with that. As yet we haven't got family commitments and I think you've got to be strong away from the club as well as at the club.

We've been married for four years and I would love children but it's such a fine line between success and failure, especially in the lower divisions, where I've played all my football. I want to give 100 per cent to football till I'm maybe 30 or 31. Joanne's got a good job and we want to secure ourselves as much as possible for the future.

I've been talking to one or two of the younger lads who've been offered one-year contracts with a bit of a wage rise, and they are not happy about it. They want signing-on fees and expenses and things like that. But those days are gone, especially at this level. Experienced players will tell you if they are offered a contract in the Third Division at the moment they are very reluctant to turn it down because things can change in two or three months. The offer might not be there any more and they've still got their mortgage to pay next year. I am financially quite sound just now, but I don't want to over-stretch myself.

Thackeray's ready smile and gentle demeanour belie his inner strength. His character has hardened along a familiar trail to the less salubrious districts of the national game. Born in Huddersfield, he returned to his home-town team after serving his apprenticeship with Manchester City.

THACKERAY

I made my League debut at Huddersfield, but had just a couple of games. I was 18½, 19, and couldn't force myself into the side permanently. Then I made a bit of a bad decision. I went to Newport County and it summed it up two weeks after I got there. We didn't get paid and the gates were locked. There are similar situations now in the Third Division. Players are wondering what's going to happen and whether their clubs are going to survive.

The good thing about Newport was that I played nearly 70 League games for them, which gave me the understanding of what professional football was about. It toughened me up and I would have been prepared if I could have gone on to bigger and better things and become a household name. It hasn't happened but I've still enjoyed my career. Newport went out of the League just before I left. I went to Wrexham for four years and then signed for Rochdale.

I could have gone to Torquay in the summer and when Rochdale found out they gave me the new two-year contract I wanted. Maybe I did use Torquay as a bit of bargaining tool but it's ruthless at this level and you've got to do it. I want to see the

Paul Butlers and Jason Peakes and Jamie Taylors do really well for themselves, because having had as much pleasure as I have, I can imagine the sort of pleasure they will get playing at a higher level. It's up to them and they've got to realise what football's all about. It's not all roses, sweetness and light. They've got to knuckle down and being here is a learning process for them.

Apart from the Cup run, seeing the younger players establishing themselves has been the big plus from our season. And they've done so against adversity. Jason is not really a youngster now but he has had to play under pressure from the supporters and staff because they expect him to do things that maybe other players can't do. I think he's grown up and had his eyes opened this year. He's had to be strong for himself and his team-mates.

I know that as skipper I have had a lot of abuse this season, but the buck stops with the captain and I don't mind. I'd rather they were shouting at me than anybody else because we have one or two younger lads who probably couldn't stand up to that. I'm captain for the players and the manager. I'm the link between them. If he wants something doing he'll call me in and I'll relay that message. If he's not happy about something but he doesn't want to give somebody an official rollicking, he'll get me to have a word and pass on the warning. I've got a lot of respect for the manager because he works tirelessly for himself, the team and the club. I know what he believes in and I believe in what he stands for, as well.

Only this week I've offered to give up the captaincy because sometimes managers want to change it. I said I'm happy doing it but sometimes a new face after a couple of years can bring a different environment to the changing room. I'm not a shouter and bawler on the pitch, but with the likes of Jason I'll have a word in their ear and say, 'Look, we need more from you here, more from you there.' That's the side the fans don't see. But the criticism doesn't bother me in the slightest. I know the few people who criticise me, I know their faces.

I know some may think the boss is soft on us, but he can be a hard man. You've got to decide if you're going to be on the lenient side, trusting your players, or go the other way. He's brought in a few more experienced players, like John Deary, Mark Stuart and Derek Hall, and he relies on them and trusts them and hopes they will guide the younger players, more than having to wield the heavy hand. It's easy to have players in and demoralise them after a heavy defeat, but that's not the manager's way. He believes they should go away and think about their performance and realise for their own sakes they have to impress him.

He knows with the older players they'll do it and when he tells us to do our own thing we'll know what we need and what's best for us. Like this morning, one or two have got knocks and little injuries, and they'll have a bath. On a day when everybody is fit the younger lads will get a ball and knock it between them for 10 minutes. The older ones do the stride-outs, the sprints, and do a good half or three-quarters of an hour session because they know, they've been through it and realise what's keeping them going. When things are not going well it's your inner will that keeps you going.

It can be a little difficult to give 100 per cent in the last two or three games of the season if nothing depends on it but I don't think it's a problem with the lads here, especially playing teams going for promotion, and the manager's happy with that. As much as he can be quite easy with us, he doesn't suffer fools gladly. The heartbeat of the club is the dressing room and he knows what's going on there. He knows when to leave it alone and when to come in and put his foot down.

Deary is a prominent figure in the dressing room, as we have seen. Creating laughs and generating team spirit are part of his stock in trade. He has been the source of even more humour after deciding to take up refereeing, a classic case of poacher turned gamekeeper. Ribbed by his team-mates for being the 'most booked and suspended player in the League', a demonic aggressor on the field, he is coy about the number of bans he has served this season. Three, is it?

'It could be,' he mutters, which also, of course, could mean it's more than three. Perhaps we've all lost count. 'I started the season with one from last season, and then with the accumulation of points . . .'

Deary is conscious his suspensions are another cause of irritation among supporters, but he, like Docherty, takes a pragmatic view of his combative style and, at the age of 33, believes he is too old a dog to be learning new tricks anyway.

DEARY
That's right. As I said when I went to the FA for my hearing, I think it was for 45 points, I said I'm approaching 600 games now and I wouldn't have played in half of them if it wasn't for my aggression. The times I have been dropped, managers have said, 'You're not competing enough.' So really, I'm caught in between.

I try to contribute to the morale. It's good in this dressing room. There's three or four of us who come out with the gags and we have a good laugh. That's helped us through and you can influence some of the younger lads in different ways. If we'd been able to keep the same team this season we'd have been in the play-off position at the very least. When I came here I said I wanted to get promotion because I'd done it with the other clubs I'd been at, Blackpool and Burnley. It would be nice to finish off my career with promotion here.

Which brings us to life after playing. But refereeing?

DEARY
Well, having seen how bad they are . . . No, only joking! The PFA are pushing for ex-players to become referees and there's a quicker route now. There was no way I was going to do refereeing if it took me 20 years to get in the Football League. But now there's a sort of short-cut, in four years, so I've applied for it. I go for a two-day course at Blackburn in July and after that I get my class 3. Then I'll have to do refereeing in local league, on Sundays next season, and progress from there. In four years I should be in the League.

257

I've also got the double glazing business so it should work out quite well. You've not got the pressure of management and coaching.

Big Willo, back from Doncaster because they didn't want to pay his wages through the summer, is both amused and intrigued by the prospect of seeing Deary in black. 'Actually I might have a look at that course. Something to do, isn't it? Get up to the Premier League, do three matches a week, a grand a week and all expenses paid, can't be bad. Mind you, it would be funny to see us clamping down on elbows and feet up. That's half our game!'

Along with his humour, Deary is renowned for his 'socialising', yet concurs with Thackeray that Docherty's liberal regime has not led to anarchy.

DEARY
The lads here are quite sensible and professional. Well, sensible in a footballer's way. I know some in our situation, with the lack of training facilities and so on, who would have really gone off the rails and gone absolutely mad. But if anybody didn't do it in the games, that would stand out a mile and the other players would want to know what was wrong. So would the manager.

Married, with a 17-month-old daughter, Deary appears to have his summer and the rest of his life mapped out. 'I'm away with the lads next week, back for two weeks, I think, then away for three weeks on a family holiday to Australia, then I've got the referee's course, and after that we start training again.'

Stuart is not so certain of his future. A somewhat incongruous voice in these parts, he is a Londoner who arrived from the schoolboy ranks with Queen's Park Rangers via Charlton, Plymouth, Ipswich on loan, Bradford and Huddersfield. Like Butler and Peake he has been offered new terms but yearns to play at a higher level. Unlike Butler and Peake, he may have blown his chance.

STUART

I'm not actually a Cockney. I'm from Hammersmith, about four or five miles from the Bow bells. I've been to almost the four corners of the country. You go where the job takes you. I've been up North six years, originally with Bradford. I've been here three years. I enjoy it up here. It's a different kind of life. I won't say it's slower, I would say it's more peaceful. You don't have to rush about so much.

I actually live in Bingley, over in Yorkshire. It's nice and quiet. You can go out with your girlfriend or your friends and you don't get bothered by anyone. A lot of the lads don't live in Rochdale itself. Jason's about 20 miles up the road from here. His local team's Burnley and because he plays for Rochdale he's not going to get noticed there, so he can go out and have a drink and just be one of the lads. I think you need that, on a Saturday night or on a Sunday, just to get away from it.

I get a bit of ribbing here for being a Londoner, but the Scousers generally get more stick than I do. I'm usually the one that's giving it out and as long as it stays that way I'm happy. I get it from my mates when I go back to London, wanting to know where

Rochdale is and saying I keep on about Rochdale going up but we always seem to do the same – start well and then fall away. But we're still trying to prove them wrong and maybe next season, if I'm still here, we'll do it.

What I've been offered for next season I don't want to take. I've told them what I want and if they come back with an offer that I think is acceptable then I'll probably accept. I know there's a couple of clubs interested but I don't know who they are. The manager says if I sign for him he'll tell me who the teams are!

As I've said to Jason and a few of the other lads, if I'd trained as hard throughout my career as I've trained this year, I'd have made more of myself. If I'm totally honest, from 17 to about 26 or 27 I didn't really put enough into the game. I went in and trained, but then went home. Never did anything extra. I had four years at Charlton, three in the top flight. I scored 13 goals in my first season playing out wide and I've let myself down, I know I have. I've not put as much into the game as the game's given me.

This season I've had a new lease of life. I think I've grown up at last, at the age of 29. That's a key to it. I'll definitely play for another five or six years because I feel fitter now than I've ever done. After playing Saturday I'll have four weeks off. I'll rest my legs but carry on doing sit-ups and press-ups and a few light weights. I want to let my body rejuvenate. I want to work on the top half of my body. I'd like to come back maybe half a stone heavier, just muscle. About 25 of us are going over to Cyprus for Jason's wedding in June so we're going to start training over there.

With all due respect to everyone else who plays in midfield, I think we've missed Peakey's imagination in midfield. He can unlock the door. He brings people into the game and can score goals, which is vital. He's the most complete midfield player I've worked with and this season he's come on a notch. He can get up and down the pitch, he's a lot quicker than people think and he's worked on the defensive side of his game. I firmly believe he could hold his own in the Premier League.

I honestly believe if, out of the blue, a miracle happened and a Premier League club came in for me now, I could play there. I am a better player, certainly mentally, than I was at 18 or 19 and I was holding my own then. I'm still quick, I can get quicker still and I'd like another crack at it. I've probably left it a bit late but I'm going to make sure I get the best out of the rest of my career.

The environment is different at every club you go to. We had a good dressing room at Charlton, and Plymouth was quite good, but I'd probably put this at the top. There's no bitterness at the club. Usually you get two or three players that some of the others don't like, but at this club, generally, everybody gets on.

Actually, Willo is a nice lad. We go for a drink or have something to eat after training and he's a lovely fella. But he's an Irishman, isn't he? Irish people tend to be hot-headed and in the heat of the moment, like in training or in a game, it's just his nature, he'll lose his rag with somebody, they have a swear at each other or square up or whatever, but it's forgotten about an hour later. You get that at football clubs, and at the end of the day you are still friends.

We know Willo's going next season but at the moment we don't know who is going to be here. It's hard to bring players in and keep them, as we are finding out. Maybe the club lacks a bit of ambition. If you want to go up a league you have to spend a bit more and maybe go into the red and take a chance. If they went up they'd get their money back. It's a difficult situation for them, though, I know.

Whatever happens in my career from now on I wouldn't swap football for any other profession. I've enjoyed it – I probably enjoyed it *too* much, when I was younger. When I was 18 and 19 I liked to go out with the lads, I liked to have a drink. I just wish I had the attitude then that I've got now. This is the best job in the world. There's not many people do the job they love for 10, 15 or 20 years. I've been lucky. I've had 12 years of it and I'm looking forward to another five or six.

It's up to me whether I do. This season has had its ups and downs, with breaking my jaw and what have you, but I've proved a lot to myself. I believe I can play at a high level and if a club wants to take a chance on me I think I'll do well.

Willo's massive frame fills the corridor as he strides back from a chat with the manager. He is as upbeat and optimistic as ever. Born in Sheffield but raised in Northern Ireland, he has played for more than a dozen clubs and already has set a target with Doncaster.

WILLIAMS
It's all set up for me to go there next season. I'm
really looking forward to it. Don't get me wrong,
I don't have a problem with the Doc. He's been
great. But the game's about opinions, isn't it? I
know people have opinions about me, and I have
my own. That's fair enough. The Doc said he didn't
want to play with a target man but then he brought
in Lancaster, who's scored one goal. I scored in my
first match with Doncaster.

I could have packed in playing long ago. I don't
have to go on. But I still love it. There's nothing
like football, just being involved with the lads and
enjoying the crack. Why should I give that up? I
know I can still do a job and you see, I'll do it next
season. I've been unlucky with injuries this season
but I'm going to get really fit this summer. I'll train
for three weeks in Marbella and come back ready
to go for the new season. And when I come back
here I'll score against Rochdale. I'm telling you,
I'll score.

For Docherty, too, next season is a challenge to be seized
by the throat. This midday, during the last week of the
1995–96 Third Division Championship of the Endsleigh
Football League, he is another tired, deflated manager.
At the age of 45 his best years in the job should be
ahead of him, but he cannot be sure. No one can. Come
next year he could be out of work, so little wonder
he is following his father's jaunty steps onto the after-
dinner speaking circuit. And yet the ambition, the self-
belief, the will to make a statement on the football field,
still burn.

DOCHERTY
I've lost none of that. Okay, so I'm a bit run down now. I've been fighting the sniffles for the last week or two. I just need a break. It's been a long season, a hard season, not only for me but for everybody here. We knew it would be. We know what to expect in our situation. But although the season's ended in disappointment, we've got plenty to look back on with pride and above all we've kept together, as a team, and the spirit now is as strong as it's ever been. I firmly believe that.

I take strength from that. After this last match I'll stay away from here for two weeks, and try to switch off if I can. That could depend on the player situation. Then I'll be in to try and sort out as much of that as I can. I'll have a week's holiday with my son, Matthew, then back in here and, if I can, take another short break before pre-season training.

It's a bit strange at this time of year, just like end of term at school, except that when the class comes back there could be a lot of new faces. At the moment we don't know. What I do know is that I'll be ready for it and they'll be ready for it, chomping at the bit. You do, don't you? We all do.

Lyons may yet be among those here next season, thanks to pressure from Frank Duffy and the Supporters' Club, who remind the management and board of their £10,000 contribution to funds. A few hastily arranged negotiations later and Docherty stitches together a compromise deal: the player is to be retained on a three-monthly contract.

Docherty can do little to bring playing matters to a satisfactory conclusion. Taylor is carried off, Thackeray limps off and the team lose 2–0 away to a Hereford side whose rise in fortunes has been as spectacular as Rochdale's fall. Docherty can only look on in envy as his counterpart, Graham Turner, the cavorting home players and nearly 6,000 delirious fans gorge themselves on the euphoria that comes with securing a place in the play-offs. Oh, what might have been. 'Today has just about summed up our season,' the Doc laments.

Rochdale's League statistics are unforgiving: played 46; won 14; drawn 13; lost 19; points 55; position 15th.

They will go off, most of them, to Majorca and drown their disappointment in San Miguel. Docherty will not be with them, after all, but doubtless will have occasion to raise a glass to the past season, and to the next one. And they will be back, possibly most of them, pursuing the fantasy all over again.

CHAPTER SIXTEEN
Final Whistle

The players fly off for their sunshine break, Docherty takes his son to the Lake District for a couple of days, all oblivious to the clouds of despair and anxiety now closing in on Spotland. An article in the *Rochdale Observer*, under the heading 'Docherty fears worst after order to trim', deepens a conviction that has been burrowing into the boardroom these past weeks – that the manager is not up to the job.

A board meeting confirms the belief and the action to be taken. The six directors, plus Keith Clegg, gather and pool their dissatisfactions and fears. A season of unfulfilled promise is one thing – they have become accustomed to that – but projected depression for the next is quite another. The directors' unease has become acute, a feeling that Docherty has lost the plot. Above all that he has lost the confidence of the town.

They wonder about his initial decision to retain Hall and Thompstone yet release Lyons; they wonder whether he has a list of players to target for next season; they wonder whether he has put in the necessary time and effort, scouting at reserve games, to have compiled such a list. There are rumours about the training schedule and one player reportedly claims they were not fit enough. Docherty admits his personal life has been 'in turmoil' and that has proved an increasingly heavy burden. His friendship with Joyce Pickles, who supplies the club their kit, ended abruptly and bitterly when she discovered his affections had been diverted towards her 21-year-old daughter, Alison. He also admits he found refuge at his local but maintains that genuine illness forced him to take days off towards the end of the season. He simply yearned for a break.

The board decide they have to make a complete break. Mace abstains, while Kilpatrick has no need to vote. The rest have reached the conclusion Docherty must go. Even Morris, loyal to Docherty throughout, concedes he can support him no more.

Docherty receives a phone call from Karen Smyth, informing him he is required to attend a board meeting the following afternoon, at 3.30, and suddenly, for the first time, he feels that thud in the pit of the stomach, that inescapable sense of foreboding. To everyone's embarrassment, he arrives along with the directors and they go through the polite ritual of shaking hands and inquiring about each other's health, when all the time Docherty is scared he is going to be sacked and the directors know he is going to be. Kilpatrick is particularly agitated because he had intended to speak to Docherty and deliver the verdict, man to man, before subjecting him to the full board. Another of the Rochdale cock-ups the chairman talks about. Kilpatrick apologises and then, with only three other directors present, Morris, Brierley and Marsh, he tells Docherty his employment is being terminated. He is offered three months' pay, £6,500, by way of compensation.

The following evening the board meet again, to talk to the man they want as Docherty's successor. He is Graham Barrow, sacked by Wigan earlier in the season. He accepts the job and is installed at the start of the following week.

MORRIS
There was a depression in the town that we couldn't afford to ignore. There's a general loss of confidence. The last thing we want, when we are trying to sell boxes and season tickets for next season, is for Mick to be saying in the local paper that we could be finding ourselves in a dangerous situation because he is being asked to operate on a skeleton staff. That smacks of making excuses before we start. But it's no different from the situation we've had for the last 16 years.

Kilpatrick, conscious this could be seen as a cosmetic exercise to induce business, insists the decision was made on footballing grounds. He is equally adamant he and his colleagues were not swayed by Docherty's private life. 'Mick phoned me about Alison and I told him, "You lucky bugger". As long as it doesn't interfere with his work, it is of absolutely no concern to me.'
The chairman pauses and then endeavours to convey the complete picture, with perspective, light and shade.

KILPATRICK
I have always tried to support Mick Docherty, despite a lot of flak directed at me as a consequence, and yes, I did say he would be our manager next

season. But I have never contended he was the best man for the job and I have to recognise that he was never universally liked or accepted on the terraces. The supporters out there always felt he was part of the Sutton regime and therefore nothing, in effect, had changed.

After a tremendous start to the season we had that horrendous run and I'm afraid you have to say that was down to bad management and not simply the injuries. Mick was offered money for players but said he didn't need it. He said there was no point unless he could have players of the quality we already had, and yet later, when he started to get a little desperate, he went for Ian Helliwell, a 33-year-old. Come on, he can't have his cake and eat it.

Then he wanted to keep Hall and Thompstone but not Lyons. We couldn't believe it. I told him we had to keep Lyons if only as a PR exercise. Otherwise there would be no point in having a youth policy if we're not seen to be keeping the best of the young players and giving them a chance. I wasn't trying to do his job and I don't claim to know better than Mick Docherty, but I do understand my responsibility as chairman of this football club. He talks of having his squad reduced to 16 or 18, but look at the ones he's had, with the likes of Williams, Shaw, Hardy, Hall and Thompstone! Mick was very good at telling people all the time about the problems he had.

There was a feeling among the directors that he hadn't done enough to prepare for next season, that he hadn't been going to as many reserve games as we believed necessary, that he didn't have a clue where to get the players he needed for next season. You then think back to what he said last year, that he wanted two new full-backs. He still hasn't got them. When we first played Hereford they were about fourth from bottom and we were right up there. In the end they made the play-offs and we were nowhere, we'd cobbed in the towel by then. I think Graham Turner made two free signings, and look at the difference.

So it wasn't any one thing that convinced us Mick had to go, it was a number of things that eventually made us see we had no alternative. There was no point putting off the decision and waiting to see what happened next season. We couldn't take that chance. We had to get a new man in and give him the best possible opportunity of getting the set-up right. Contrary to what some may think, we had not offered Graham Barrow the job before we sacked Docherty. We were obviously aware he was available and having given Mick our decision we then made arrangements to speak to Graham. We feel he is right for the job. Time will tell.

It was unpleasant sacking Mick, but it had to be done. In many respects I've got a lot of time for him and overall he represented the club well. On reflection, though, perhaps he is a number two after all and was never cut out to be a number one. Again, time will tell.

Appropriately heavy, sullen skies shroud the moors towards Burnley as Docherty again seeks solace at his watering hole. Commentary of England's match in China provides an exotic backdrop to his version of this local melodrama. Inside this symbolically windswept outpost, he sits near the fire, cosy and protected, clutching a pint of lager, friends and confidants providing buffers either side. He is wearing jeans, an open-neck shirt and trainers. He is clean-shaven and looks well enough; subdued yet not sombre.

DOCHERTY
I'm all right, considering. I've got some good friends here, good people. They've looked after me when I've needed it, given me a lot of support. They can't understand what's happened to me. No one I've spoken to can. It came right out of the blue. I'd not had any idea, not a sniff. I told them after the last match I wanted to get away from it and switch off for a week, and that's what I did. Took Matthew up to the Lakes, saw my dad, just sort of wound down, which I needed.

Then I got a call from Karen the following Monday asking me if I was going in on the Tuesday. I said I was because I wanted to sort out one or two new offers for some of the players out of contract, which I was going to discuss with them on the Wednesday. As soon as she said I was wanted at a board meeting at 3.30 on the Tuesday, which I'd never known before, I had a feeling something wasn't right. I asked her if she was going to be there, as normal, taking the minutes, and Karen, lovely naive girl that she is, said funnily enough she wasn't. I was pretty sure then what was happening. I couldn't understand it, but it all pointed to the sack.

When I turned up there I saw the directors and

I'm shaking them by the hand thinking 'You all know I'm sacked'. Sure enough, the chairman told me and then said he wanted all the directors to tell me why. But to be honest, I still don't understand why. I got all this about not buying players when the money was there, but I didn't want to spend for the sake of it. Then the retained list. Hall I wasn't decided about, but then said I would release. Thompstone is versatile and that is useful when you've got a small squad. I gather they've both now been released. Lyons, I told them, was lightweight. I also told the chairman that making decisions like that was surely my shout, but I have to say he, and Rod Brierley, always gave me the impression they felt they could manage the team better than me.

It's true I didn't have a long list of players for next season but I had been to a sufficient number of matches and told them so, and I had earmarked people to take over from the likes of Butler and Peake. There was no point having a long list at this stage. The released lists are out at the beginning of June and if all the players I'd wanted to stay had stayed I would have been able to take on only one or two more anyway.

All this about wanting to sell boxes and season tickets makes you think that they just want to freshen it up a bit, that they feel they have to every now and then, to get publicity, and what better way than getting a new manager? I don't remember using the word 'dangerous' when I talked about the situation for next season but I did feel we could be left short again and in saying so I was just being honest.

I thought that in the circumstances I'd done a reasonably good job. I certainly think that if they weren't totally happy they could at least have given me another shot, with a full squad again, until November or December. But they'd made up their minds and that was it. I stood up, shook them all by the hand again, thanked them for giving me the opportunity to manage Rochdale, wished them all well for the future, and told them I thought they were wrong. I left them with a bit of dignity. There was no acrimony. Inside, though, I was feeling sick. I'd gone there originally a couple of days a week, helping out, for £50, expenses really to travel from Blackpool. I'd put a hell of a lot into it. Now I was out. At least they agreed to let me keep the car for a week or so.

I came here afterwards and got blasted. Out of my brains. The people here took my keys off me and sent me home in a taxi. That's the way they look after me. The directors talk about selling boxes, but there's a bloke in here has one and he says he's not renewing it. He's disgusted. So are the players. Every man jack of them rang me. They're gutted. Peakey threw up – literally. Butler says that's it, he's definitely leaving now. Mind you, I said to him, 'Come on, Butts, you were going anyway'. Still, it's nice to hear things like that. I've had calls of commiseration from other people in the game – Joe Royle, for instance. People in the game are good like that and I don't have a problem with Graham Barrow. He's a good lad and I wish him well. But he's got a thankless task.

I can't help wonder whether my private life had